Magic of the Sixties

Magic of the Sixties

GENE ANTHONY

Gibbs Smith, Publisher
Salt Lake City

First Edition
08 07 06 05 04   5 4 3 2 1

Published by
Gibbs Smith, Publisher
P.O. Box 667
Layton, Utah 84041

Orders: 1.800.748.5439
www.gibbs-smith.com

Designed by Steven Rachwal
Printed and bound in Hong Kong

Library of Congress Cataloging-in-Publication Data
Anthony, Gene.
  Magic of the sixties / Gene Anthony.—1st ed.
    p. cm.
  ISBN 1-58685-378-3
  1. United States—History—1961-1969. 2. Popular culture—
United States—History—20th century. 3. Counterculture—
United States—History—20th century. I. Title.
E841.A58 2004
979.4'6053'0222—dc22
                              2004012235

To Anna, Joshua, Maggy, and Paul

Arriving in Style

At the beginning of 1964, I had been out of the country for eighteen months, freelancing for *TimeLife* and *Playboy,* in Rio de Janeiro. John F. Kennedy had been assassinated. The sight of green camouflaged battle tanks rolling down Avenida Atlantica, in Copacabana, cooled my enthusiasm for the expatriate lifestyle and energized my departure for home.

Rio de Janeiro to New York by ship takes two weeks. I arrived on a Hudson River pier with my wife, Maggy, all but broke, but well relaxed, with a dark tropical tan and lots of baggage, which included a parrot and a dog. Squeezing all of us into a Checker cab, I headed across town for the Algonquin Hotel.

It was a fortunate beginning. My Brazilian favela dog, Winnie, had taken that moment to relieve herself on the doorman's shoe as we wrestled with heavy suitcases and assorted boxes. O'Leary, a blue-crested Amazon parrot, was stentoriously singing, "My Wild Irish Rose," and to my chagrin, an audience was forming. I didn't have a reservation and had only limited funds. But this story is about faith!

Fortunately, the Algonquin accepts a little commotion with arriving guests. Alec Wilder, the Broadway director, came out the front door to see who was causing a crowd. Tall, well groomed, with thinning gray hair, he offered his card and inquired: "Are you someone? You have to be someone special to make an entrance like that!" Ten minutes later a bellman was at my door with a basket of flowers, cheese, and fruit. A card read "Welcome to New York!"

Above: Author Gene Anthony arrived in style in New York City with lots of baggage, a blue-crested Amazon parrot, and a Brazilian favela dog named Winnie.
Left: Sexuality was openly expressed in the clubs of Rio; Gene Anthony had been living in Rio for eighteen months as a freelance photographer for TimeLife and Playboy.

Serendipity

Overcoming life's temporary pitfalls is a matter of optimism and trust. My mother's favorite maxim resonates: "Life is just a matter of solving problems!"

In the sixties, a freelance photographer could call a magazine picture-editor, and with the right story, sell it over the phone and get a guarantee, plus an advance, wired by Western Union. The magic lay in the story.

The following morning, in a coffee shop, a discarded copy of *Variety* had what I needed: "Nude Swim is SRO in Frisco." The spirits heard my plea. "Nude swim?" Nudity had never been accepted in public clubs; Cannes, perhaps, but not in San Francisco.

The New York Public Library was almost around the corner, where I found the *San Francisco Chronicle* with a recent column by the nonpareil columnist Herb Caen:

"When the topless bathing suit appeared last month, the Condor's Carol Doda, who was already descending five times nightly on an elevator-rigged piano, modeled a topless swimsuit and the club had its biggest gross in its 12-year history. . . . I tellya, this topless swimsuit thing is getting out of hand—or should that be phrased more delicately? Last night Carol, the 'Swim' dancer at Gino del Prete's Condor, did her act sans bra, and the joint was immediately jammed

Right: The "psychedelic lady" expresses both the sexual openness and the creativity of the flower children.

Above: Nudity was popular as an expression of freedom and could always get out the media if the hippies had an issue to raise.
Right: Columnist Herb Caen found much to say about the new nudist movement in San Francisco.

to the rafters. A rival's Off Broadway got wind of these developments, whereupon his 'Champagne' dancer, Dee Dee, shed the top of her bikini for her next show—and then his joint was jammed. North Beach is fast becoming Mammary Lane, and I have a feeling the next words you hear will be uddered by Police Chief Tom Cahill."

That was the story I needed. Buoyed with enthusiasm, I phoned *Playboy Magazine* in Chicago. I had worked for *Playboy* a couple of times; in Rio I contributed to a "Girls of Rio" spread. After explaining my thoughts about a "Frisco Topless" story, to *Playboy* picture editor Vince Tajiri, he gave me a two-week guarantee. Once more, my guardian spirits had saved me from the brink.

**Below, left: Body painting became a popular new art form.
Below, right: Nudity on the beaches was common in the San Francisco area.**

Back in California

California enjoys a special magnetism, and San Francisco has maintained a frontier spirit. The city's physical appeal, and historical acceptance of new beginnings, has always spawned controversial movements. This has given support to the adage that the Bay Area is a crucible for the bizarre and the weird. The city continues to maintain that reputation. Only now, in the new millennium, the weirdness and weirdos of the sixties have morphed into innovation and innovators.

  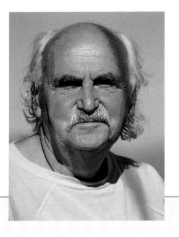  

I was born Eugene Jensen Anthony across the bay from San Francisco, in Berkeley. When I was seven, an after-school photography demonstration at Oxford Elementary School was the spark that started my career. The sight of a photographic image emerging on a piece of photo paper is still etched in my memory. My mother gave me a little black Bakelite box Kodak Brownie camera, and after that, I began to see the world as a series of images that I wanted to photograph.

Then there is my passion for all things nautical, cultivated by reading the extraordinary voyages of Magellan and Francis Drake, and books by Joseph Conrad, Joshua Slocum, Richard Henry Dana, E. M. Forster, and all the others. During WWII my mother worked as a welder in a Kaiser Shipyard in Richmond, building Liberty and Victory ships. Eventually, after getting my seaman's papers, I joined the SUP (Sailors Union of the Pacific) and went to sea in some of those ships, as a deck sailor.

Beginning in 1953, I shipped out in the Merchant Marine aboard American President Lines, troop carriers, Matson passenger liners, Moore McCormick, Grace, and Pacific Far East cargo vessels. These had much the same routine: two and three month voyages to Hawaii, Asia, and South America. On the beach, in San Francisco, my head was turned by the Beat Generation, led by Allen Ginsberg and Larry Ferlinghetti. Michael McClure, Kenneth Rexroth, Bob Kaufman, and Brother Antoninus, as well

Above: Lawrence Ferlinghetti, Kenneth Rexroth, Jean Varda, Bob Kaufman, and Allen Ginsberg were among the many poets on the Haight-Ashbury scene.
Below: This young man chills out on his bike in the Haight-Ashbury neighborhood.

as art students who hung out in the shadow of Coit Tower, on upper Grant Avenue, in North Beach, or at the California School of Fine Arts (now The San Francisco Art Institute). A hangout was The Place, a sometime headquarters for my newfound universe. I stood out, but didn't realize how much at the time. I was the kid who wore the hand-sewn silver gray silk shirts, slacks, and handmade shoes from Hong Kong, who was always taking pictures with a Nikon camera kept in a WWII gas mask bag hanging from his shoulder.

The Victorian homes in the Haight-Ashbury neighborhood became the center of many social happenings.

The Blackhawk, a jazz club at Turk and Hyde Streets, was another haunt. The owner Helen Noga, who discovered Johnny Mathis, stood at the door and "let me in." Stan Getz, Dinah Washington, Errol Garner, Brubeck, Anita O'Day—all the jazz stars came through the Blackhawk. I also met Ralph J. Gleason, the *San Francisco Chronicle* jazz columnist. I reciprocated my free passes with wheels of cheese from Argentina and ivory chess sets from the Orient.

North Beach

From its first days in business, Café Trieste, on Grant Avenue in North Beach, became the Well for the North Beach Beats, serving my imported Argentine queso on sandwiches. Farther up Grant Avenue, the Coexistence Bagel Shop took top billing on a Gray Line tour of Beatnik territory. Maggie Reiff organized her North Beach friends, hired a bus, and conducted a Beatnik March on the city's posh Union Square, the Beatnik Tour of the Capitalist Wasteland. Prose and poetry were the features

inside a converted garage, the Six Gallery, where Allen Ginsberg had the first public reading of *Howl.* Jazz and blues with poetry by Ginsberg and Ferlinghetti went down at The Cellar, a jazz club under Green Street, owned by Bill Weijohn. There was live jazz and Lenny Bruce at the Jazz Workshop on Broadway. All these were places where my chum-chaw from exotic far Pacific lands was eagerly embraced. A lot was happening around the city; there was a buzz of excitement all over town.

Between trips to sea, I attended photography classes at the California School of Fine Arts on the slopes of Russian Hill in North Beach. Ansel Adams taught his Zone System and printing techniques, and Dorothea Lange encouraged me to stay with photography. Those were the days of Richard Diebenkorn and Elmer Bischoff, Sam Francis, John Altoon, Joan Brown, and Ernest Mutt.

In the Pacific, my ships stopped at Hawaii, Japan, Okinawa, Manila, and Hong Kong, where I took photographs that I could sell on my return home. Photographs depicting the fast-changing face of Asia were in demand. After one particular voyage, a friend told me that *Playboy Magazine* was looking for pictures of musicians. By chance, Frank Sinatra had a matinee performance in San Francisco that weekend; I managed to get a seat in front of the stage and shot a roll of black-and-white film. When *Playboy* bought one of my photographs, I changed careers.

This photo of Frank Sinatra was sold to **Playboy Magazine.** Its purchase was the jumping-off point for Gene Anthony in a long and successful photography career.

City Lights

"Unscrew the locks from the doors!

Unscrew the doors themselves from their jambs!"

— Howl

A significant influence on the reputation

of San Francisco's literary renaissance and the Summer of Love was the leading role played by Allen Ginsberg and his book of poems *Howl.* Thirty-two-year-old Ginsberg was the flamboyant literary renegade poet whose international reputation was ignited by the seizure of his first published book of poetry, *Howl and Other Poems,* and the subsequent trial. Critics had rendered *Howl* the fomenter for raising issues on the minds of young people searching for their own voice. It was a 5 x 6-inch, 75-cent volume of forty-four pages, published by Lawrence Ferlinghetti's City Lights Publishing Company.

Lines such as the following unsettled the establishment: "I saw the best minds of my generation destroyed by madness, starving hysterical naked..." and "stained shrieks of frantic defiance."

Their response: "We have had smoking attacks on the civilization before, ironic or murderous or suicidal. We have not had this particular variety of anguished anathema-hurling in which the poet's revulsion is expressed with the single-minded frenzy of a raving madwoman."

City Lights was the first all-paperback bookstore in U.S. and became literary ground zero in San Francisco.

After seizure and impoundment of *Howl,* the incident immediately became a call-to-arms over the issue of free speech. It created a literary sensation. It was immediately debated around the country and put Allen Ginsberg and *Howl* into the national spotlight and the American consciousness.

"S.F. Poet's Latest Book Too Earthy For U.S. Customs," said the *San Francisco Examiner* headline in March 1957. The page-two news story said that U.S. Customs and the San Francisco Police had seized 520 copies of *Howl* for being obscene.

"Customs Seizes Poetry—Not Fit For Children" was a *San Francisco Chronicle* headline. "It's disgusting, the words and the sense of the writing is depraved and obscene," declared Collector of Customs, Chester MacPhee. "You certainly wouldn't want young children to read it."

"It's filth, not fit for young people," intoned Captain William Hanrahan of the San Francisco Police Juvenile Bureau, while arresting my friend Shig Murao who was the City Lights bookstore clerk, when the cops decided to arrest someone. "When I say a filthy book I don't mean suggestive, I mean filthy words that are vulgar," said Captain Hanrahan in a louder voice. Someone asked if he

would also confiscate the Bible. Poet Kenneth Rexroth assured reporters that "*Howl* is the confession of faith of the generation which is going to be running the world in the late '90s."

Should *Howl* be seized? Ferlinghetti had first inquired whether or not the American Civil Liberties Union would take up the issue. As it turned out, when the book was seized it became the hot new topic of conversation among poets and writers across the country. In court proceedings, a team of eminent criminal lawyers took on the case pro bono, and the trial lasted throughout the summer. In the end, eloquent faculty members from the University of California and San Francisco State took their turn addressing the differences between hard-core pornography and writing judged to be social speech.

A "redeeming social importance" became the new litmus test for the courts. The effect was to embolden a new wave

Allen Ginsberg wrote *Howl and Other Poems*, a book that sparked a national debate on literature, pornography, and free speech.

City Lights bookstore was a small but crowded literary center in North Beach. It was center stage in the controversy over Allen Ginsberg's Howl.

of writers and readers. It legitimized behavior and encouraged more freedoms that were seen as more permissiveness.

"Cops Don't Allow No Renaissance Here," was the *San Francisco Examiner's* acknowledgement of the emerging North Beach literary movement, whose participants were becoming known as Beats. In 1956, Herb Caen called the dozen or so North Beach literary figures Beatnik—in reference to the Soviet spacecraft, *Sputnik I,* then successfully orbiting the earth. The term *Beat* is actually from New York, taken from the down and dirty, exhausted look that drifters and addicts took on, characterized by Jack Kerouac's *On the Road,* which called them beatific, beats, the Beat Generation. Ginsberg and Kerouac, along with William Burroughs, were friends in New York. They were hostile to materialism and conformity, which they expressed in their work. In 1955, Ginsberg migrated west and became a figure in the "San Francisco Poetry Renaissance" about the time Lawrence Ferlinghetti opened City Lights. Later, the issue of the trial and the sideshow that went with it became the opening salvos on a national debate about obscenity. It was the new challenge by youth.

Opened in 1955, City Lights is a small but always crowded literary center in North Beach. It was established as the first all-paperback bookstore in the United States and became the literary ground zero in San Francisco. City Lights carries a good stock of literary quarterlies, dozens of foreign imprints, and periodicals. The significance of being the first all-paperback bookstore in the U.S. should not be lost. Until the late fifties, underground books that

The Grateful Dead are one of the most enduring cultural icons of the sixties.

The Jefferson Airplane at the Fillmore in 1967.

would attempt to "subvert public morality" were published in small, plain, blank-cover paperback editions that wouldn't excite the book police too much. *Lady Chatterley's Lover* and Henry Miller's *Tropics* were first sold with blank covers and found only in Paris. Establishing an all-paperback bookstore was considered a very daring act and helped bring the issue of literary censorship to prominence.

This was the McCarthy era, and *Howl* generated considerable support around the country for voicing dissent against censorship. That spring Senator Joseph McCarthy died, ending a haunting time in America. The country was just waking up and beginning to discuss the First Amendment. Poets and writers and other artists were searching for truth while the establishment was howling its hypocrisy. Ginsberg's admission of his communism and homosexuality in his work was too much for the old guard to sustain. Ironically, it didn't matter what the old guard wanted anymore, because Ginsberg and the emerging counterculture were talking to the youth.

The Emerging Counterculture of the Sixties

These were some of the headlines, songs, bands, buzzwords, and hot topics at the tip of the new wave:

"Mr. Tambourine Man"
"Vietnam War Protester Immolates Self"
"Selma"
"Soviet Cosmonaut in Space"
"LSD-25"
"25,000 American Troops in Vietnam"
"Teach-In"
"Marine Divisions in Vietnam"
"A Ticket to Ride"
"Do you believe in Magic?"
"Red Dog Saloon"
"Help!"
"A Tribute to Dr. Strange"
"East Coast Power Failure"
"Malcolm X Shot"
"Gilligan's Island"
"The Rolling Stones"
"Downtown"

"Watts"
"Yesterday"
"The times they are a changing."
"You don't know what's happening,
   do you, Mr. Jones?"
The Birds
The Charlatans
The Grateful Dead
The Jefferson Airplane
Quick Silver Messenger Service
Family Dog, Lovin' Spoonful
Great Society, Paul Revere and the Raiders
Country Joe and the Fish
The Only Alternative
The Thirteenth Floor Elevator
Mothers of Invention
It's a Beautiful Day
Big Brother and the Holding Company

The Magic Bus

About this time the Kesey bus "Furthur" happened along.

Ken Kesey was both Pied Piper and ringmaster of the Merry Prankster circus that crossed the country aboard a 1939 International Harvester school bus, creating a magical wake that had a profound effect on the emerging counterculture.

In 1964, Ken Kesey, author of *One Flew Over the Cuckoo's Nest*, literary star and media celebrity, was riding a crest of writer's euphoria after the considerable success of *Cuckoo's Nest*. Considering all his options, he decided to set out on a journey with friends, from La Honda to La Honda, by way of Florida, a visit to the New York World's Fair, and a side trip to Canada. In general he wanted to promote his book, see some people along the way, and make a movie of it. First he bought a bus, named it "Furthur," outfitted it with the latest tape recorders, sound equipment, a 16mm Bolex and 16mm Arroflex with a 400-foot film magazine, some costumes, some musical instruments, and a few flags. Then he headed out on an approximate course of 070 degrees.

On the Bus

Kesey's friends aboard the bus were called the Merry Pranksters. Kesey was the "Chief" or "Swashbuckler." Some of the other names of the travelers included "Intrepid Traveler," "Speed Demon," "Speed Limit," "Dis-mount," "Hardly Visible," "Mal Function," "Hassler," "Brother Charlie," "Highly Charged," "Doris Delay," "Sometimes Missing," "Generally Famished," "Mountain Girl," "Gretchen Fetchin," "Slime Queen," and "Stark Naked."

Ken Kesey's "Magic Bus" made a national sensational with its tour.

Painted in psychedelic
patterns and colors, the
bus, named "Further,"
carried the Merry Band
of Pranksters on their
tour.

At the urging of "Intrepid Traveler" Ken Babbs, the crew was encouraged to create pranks as part of the agenda, embodying the Kesey program of spontaneity and authenticity. Hence, the Prankster moniker. Pranksters carried out the scheme wearing elaborate costumes and painting themselves and the bus in Day-Glo fluorescent colors. Adding more confidence to their enterprise, the destination box at the front of the bus read "Furthur." Spray painted across the bumper in silver paint was the secret word "Magic." The rear of the bus had a sign that read "Caution—Weird Load."

One prank get-rich-quick scheme was a plan to exploit the Prankster name recognition, selling "Official Prankster" credentials, with an illuminated nineteenth-century certificate design, at $2 a pop. The authentic Prankster diplomas—the ones for the original two dozen Pranksters who made the trip to the New York World's Fair—have an additional last line that makes them authentic valued originals: "Never trust a Prankster."

Ron Bevort describes the trip this way in his book *On the Bus:* "You have to realize, that this was an unpleasant trip. It was noisy and chaotic on the bus. Some people wanted to be left alone and others wanted to keep sticking a camera in everyone's face. On top of that, it was hot. This was summer and we were going through the South. We couldn't get cool. We couldn't stop sweating. At times we couldn't hear anything but the noise of the bus. The most memorable experiences are often the most unpleasant ones."

Prankster George Walker worked with a hand-held

16 mm Bolex, and Prankster Tom Hagen, the chief cinematographer, operated an Arroflex 16 mm with a 400-foot film magazine. They shot fifty hours of film—everything that moved during the journey. They were brave souls and shot in the French way, i.e., *cinema vérité* sans shooting script. That was an error. Once they were back home, Kesey couldn't make sense of any of the film. He proceeded to preview the saga for friends as an art project in progress. There was a party at the California School of Fine Arts (Art Institute), complete with Zack Stewart repelling down the school tower, where Kesey was advised to cut the film into five reels and play them on five projectors at the same time.

The Acid Tests were presented by Ken Kesey and his Merry Band of Pranksters. These wild parties included light shows, sound, music, and film clips from the Magic Bus tour. The Acid Tests were the prototype for the Fillmore's live rock 'n' roll concerts.

The Acid Tests

When I first met Ken Kesey, out at San Francisco State, he had already returned from his national tour and was stopping at colleges and universities. Kesey wasn't the high-energy, freaky character that I had expected. Rather, he was somber and laid back. A solidly built, blue-eyed, high school wrestling champion, Ken wore a seaman's boson's whistle, the kind used in sailing ships to signal orders to sailors working high in the topsails. Ken found the whistle handy for communicating commands on the bus through the cacophony of sounds from radios, competing conversations, horns, and medicated companions. Rumors about his adventures were giving Kesey a near-mythical reputation that had a certain legitimacy because of his authorship. *Cuckoo's Nest* is about craziness.

The Acid Tests were receiving attention from the *San Francisco Chronicle's* Ralph Gleason: "Ken Kesey, author of 'One Flew Over the Cuckoo's Nest,' is presenting his Merry Band of Pranksters, tomorrow night at the Fillmore Auditorium, in a program he finds impossible to describe in words. The happening is called 'The Acid Test' and includes lights, sound, and music. Kesey says that he is expressing himself through 'The Acid Test' these days and not through the more orthodox methods of fiction. 'I write in this thing so you can see it as it happens,' he says. The Fillmore Auditorium happening is scheduled to go on all night," *San Francisco Chronicle,* December 18, 1965.

An Acid Test at the Fillmore was held a few days after New Year's. It was a warm-up to the Trips Festival two weeks later. The kids wore costumes, painted their faces, and bounced golden balloons into flickering high-frequency strobe lights. It hurt one's eyes just to look at it. In fact, a cop that had wandered into the auditorium decided that the flickering lights had to stop. Strobe flashing light was dangerous, he said.

Kids wore costumes, painted their faces, and danced all night in the flickering lights. It was the participation of the crowd that was new and revolutionary.

Mountain Girl at the Love-In.

Bouts with the Law

A few days after his Fillmore Acid Test, Kesey was in court to answer an arrest warrant issued the year before for a pot bust. This succeeded in giving him a certain Robin Hood–like aura. Kesey pled guilty for possession and escaped a long prison term "by the skin of his teeth" after a verbal tongue-lashing from the judge. He got three year's probation on condition that he use no narcotics, marijuana, or other dangerous drug prohibited by law. The judge also forbade him to associate with any person engaged in that type of activity. In addition, Kesey was ordered not to sponsor any gathering where minors were present without approval of his probation officer, and was issued a $1,500 fine. "Your record is clean," said the judge, "otherwise you'd be going to state prison." The state wasn't consistent with its marijuana laws. Some counties would send violators away for four to five years for possession of a roach.

Outrageousness rolled on. Twenty-four hours after receiving orders from the superior court judge "not to associate with your business associates on any kind of social level," Kesey was busted again. The *San Francisco Examiner* headline read, "Author Ken Kesey has New Bout with the Law!" The newspaper lead read, "A raid on a roof garden 'business conference' sent novelist Kenneth Kesey and a stunning brunette to jail early today." The *San Francisco Chronicle* said, "Cops Find Kesey—Rooftop Drama." The "stunning brunette" was Carolyn Adams, known to her friends as "MG" or "Mountain Girl." She was described in the *Chronicle* as "a lanky beauty with long pigtails, white tennis shoes and pink shoelaces." Kesey was handcuffed, and he and Mountain Girl were taken to city prison and booked for possession of marijuana. Kesey was additionally charged with assaulting a police officer and resisting arrest. Poor Kesey, he couldn't make a move without the press looking on.

Left: Ken Kesey, author of One Flew Over the Cuckoo's Nest, was a literary star, media celebrity, and ringleader of the Merry Band of Pranksters.
Below: Ron Bevort with the Pranksters at the first Appeal Party, held in an old warehouse in San Francisco.

Kesey got out on bail, and I caught up with him at Margo St. James's place. Margo was a famed Nob Hill madam who later created Coyote. The press was anxious to find Ken, and Margo had been a splendid person to inform me of his whereabouts. He posed for his photograph in front of one of Margo's paintings that seemed appropriate.

In general, Kesey found the authorities angry with him for any manifestation of rebellion, especially his well-publicized road trip. "Well," said Kesey, "they haven't seen anything yet." And LSD would be legal for another year.

From Ron Bevort, a.k.a. "Hassler"

"Basically, Ken Kesey's Acid Tests grew out of 'Happenings' that were first conceived by poets Allen Ginsberg, Gerd Stern, and painter Steve Durkee in 1957. 'Happenings' were also developed and produced at San Francisco State. Happenings were created more as an art show. Live music was not part of the program. You could bash a car fender with a hammer, swing on a chair suspended from the ceiling, climb a rope ladder. Gerd Stern, a poet and part-time public relations man, believed that audience participation would render an event a greater success. Gerd and Steve Durkee had also tried to exploit the refraction potential of plastic holograms that symbolized their new art form. The spectrum of color that was dispersed by the holograms, a product of the developing plastics industry, captivated people. Steve Durkee created large collage hologram images that were later displayed on the walls at the Happenings. Ken Kesey told me that he had talked with Durkee and Ginsberg about their Happenings, and had built on the concept, which he would call Acid Tests."

Penny Lane Parties

Kesey's Penny Lane parties were part of the underground rumor circuit. His involvement with LSD research at the Palo Alto Veterans Hospital was also talked about. Kesey said that he was trying to re-create the acid experience, which was about letting go and being aware of new dimensions, exploring new frontiers of the mind. Kesey said that he wanted to re-create the universe he found on acid, without acid.

A couple of the parties were also held in Kesey's new home, in the hills above Palo Alto, La Honda. In 1965, the small white stucco house was on six acres of land in the country. The back of the house extended to the surrounding county watershed property. It was the perfect place for Ron Boise's Electric Thunder sculptures of welded metal depicting the Kama Sutra. His art created a scandal, especially the piece that showed a man and woman having oral sex. Mobile sculptures hung from the trees next to Ken Babbs' speakers. The Hell's Angels were invited to party with Kesey, who was hopeful that LSD could calm down the Angels and alter their propensity for the negative lifestyle.

Ken Babbs set up several loudspeakers in the trees. He

Above: The first Appeal Party. Kids were invited to wear costumes and bring gadgets to play with. Left: Ken Kesey at the Acid Graduation party that quickly morphed as the Trips Festival and then into shows at the Fillmore.

connected them to his electronic sound synthesizers, passing sound from speaker to speaker, and producing his version of the sound of Psychedelia. These sound tricks later helped Don Bukala create his sound synthesizers that were used at the Trips Festival. (Let me note here that there are many books to be read about the Trips Festival, documented by others in attendance. Tom Wolfe's *The Electric Kool-Aid Acid Test* is one. I was little more than a spectator with a camera, getting only a glimpse. Much of the time I had little understanding of what was really happening, except to say that people were enjoying themselves, participating in the program, and having a lot of fun.)

Rallies for peace, love, and compassion embodied the spirit of the flower children.

Demonstrations and Rallies

Protests have been around since before the days of Troy.

The San Francisco Bay Area sixties protests were made up of students and mothers and fathers and other folks who gathered at street intersections, parks, and landmarks to march and express their feelings and concerns about the war in Vietnam. They also wanted to bring attention to women's rights, black power, and other issues.

Demonstrations and rallies brought together people of like mind; they were about people meeting people, people being people. For much of the decade, weekend protests were part of the student culture that would often end up at a rock 'n' roll dance concert. People's lives intersected at protests. A long march was a place to camp out and meet new friends.

Word about protests was passed about on radio, in underground and daily newspapers, and notices on school bulletin boards, or on tables manned by students. Signs and hand-outs were created and set out in stacks to take. People marched for miles. There was even a Walk to Moscow, all in the name of peace.

Blue-suited Berkeley police took on a military style, wearing the armament and protective gear of Marines ready to battle against Flower Power. When the police realized that the enemy was tame and was playing some kind of new game, the press loved it and wanted more. So the kids responded with outrageousness that included nudity. The expression made by walking nude or barefoot caught the moment. In San Francisco a group of nude protesters climbed aboard a cable car. There is the story that a heckler was being rude at an Allen Ginsberg poetry reading.

Peace rallies and other demonstrations are synony-mous with the sixties. College-age kids marched for peace, to end the war in Vietnam, for women's rights, blacks rights, and gay rights.

As his retort, Allen began taking off his clothes until eventually he was completely nude. That was 1959, I'm told. Nudity was always good to get some press and, of course, "dirty words" were an attention getter.

At the end of the decade protests were a bright patch on the quilted fabric of the sixties.

Sometimes demonstrators clashed with the police who were called in to keep peace and order in Bay Area streets.

The craziness of the sixties ran the gamut. Left: Phyllis Wilner rides down Haight Street screaming "Freeeee!" Below: A street audience forms to enjoy a demonstration.

Fashions incorporated everything from beads, long skirts, Native American costumes, and flowers to the American flag.

Now Day parade. Poet Michael McClure is on the right wearing sunglasses, and writer Richard Bravtigan is in the white hat.

Now Day—the death of money now—on Haight Street was a spontaneous demonstration that included the San Francisco Mime Troupe, the Diggers, and the Hell's Angels.

Demonstrations to end
the war in Vietnam
drew huge crowds
throughout the sixties.

People rallied to express their political views and to spread the cry for peace.

Above: A boy escapes a policeman's club by taking refuge in a tree.

Left: Protests involved the whole family.

Right: Young men and women marched together in protest against the war.

Far right: Additional law enforcement was called in to keep the crowds under control.

OCT. 15
16

DAYS OF INTERNATIONAL

PROTEST

AGAINST THE

WAR IN VIETNAM

Above: H. Rap Brown was a frequent speaker for
black power and the Black Panthers.
Facing: Many people spoke out passionately
against the war in Vietnam.

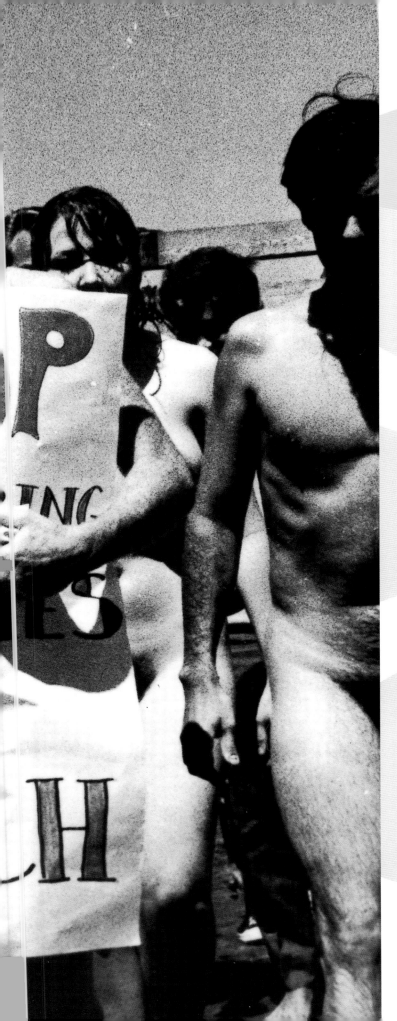

**Nudity was all about
expressing yourself.
People marched for
more nude beaches.**

Sex

From the outset of the counterculture, nudity was never a matter of sensuality.

Nudity had to do with expressing who you were. It was about nakedness, as expressed by Allen Ginsberg. Nudity was a matter of poetic nakedness and candor. Nudity symbolized having the integrity to stand before the world—open, direct, and not afraid to speak the truth.

Nakedness was expressed in many ways. There was the nude beach at San Gregario Beach, a few miles south of San Francisco. There was also the Sexual Freedom League, a small group who understood the humor of pushing the establishment's buttons and had nude parties. Either way, it made for great camera. Soon enough the word got out and nudity became eye candy and was called Topless.

Still, the concept of poetic nakedness was important to many people. Everything about sex was well suppressed before the sixties. Life in America had changed drastically in the years since WWII ended. The country was becoming urban and educated. Studies said women had become more sexually demanding; they wanted quality—not quantity—and there was more of an emphasis on togetherness. *Time Magazine* reported that the modern couple were together much more than they used to be and were concerned with having common interests.

Playboy caused a considerable stir when first published in 1953. People were falling down in shock that such perversion could be tolerated in America. But the courts relented. *Playboy* was followed by *Penthouse* and the rush was on. Given the free reign offered by the courts, sex became an industry in North Beach and began sprouting up as an industry across the country.

By 1965 San Francisco boasted thirty-six massage par-
lors, twenty-five porn theaters, sex encounter groups,
thriving escort services, and a bondage and discipline club
with seven hundred Bay Area members. North Beach was
the undisputed epicenter of the topless, nudity, and sex
frenzy in America.

As nudity was playing its role in the hippie community,
my concern was how to get photographs. In the end, I
would have to participate. High school bulletin boards
around town had been a traditional source for underground information. For a freelance photographer it was
crucial to be in touch.

From the topless movement to the Sexual Freedom League, nudity
was causing a stir. Nude parties became popular and the counterculture cry was "make love not war."

Nude Parties

Nude parties were the new "thing," another symbolic protest against middle-class hypocrisy. The rumors of these parties caught everyone's attention, so to round out my curiosity I went to a few. Later I invited my friends so that I would feel less embarrassed. Nude parties were not organized sex. The nude parties I attended were held in an apartment near Twin Peaks, the upper Haight. Nude parties were a new stage of exploration of sex in general. The Pill had just arrived, and with plenty of female pulchritude. A counterculture rally cry was "Make Love Not War."

Nudity was selling well. It was catching the public's attention, and the magazines couldn't get enough sexual overtones. People talked about the West Coast's wondrous bare market. The San Gregario beach scene had an effect on several groups who focused on the absurdity of laws forbidding naked bodies. It made an interesting counterpoint to the war protests and was part of the fun. For a time it became a contest between different people trying to be seen as more outrageous and liberal. This was a time when Lenny Bruce was getting arrested for using too many four-letter words in his nightclub monologues. But whenever he got arrested, the most prominent in the arts—Theodore Reik, Norman Mailer, James Baldwin, and many others—came to his rescue, describing him as on par with Swift and Twain. Another great comedian was Dick Gregory. Comics were getting national press for exploring forbidden words and topics, but the time between contention and acceptance seemed very short.

The hungry i

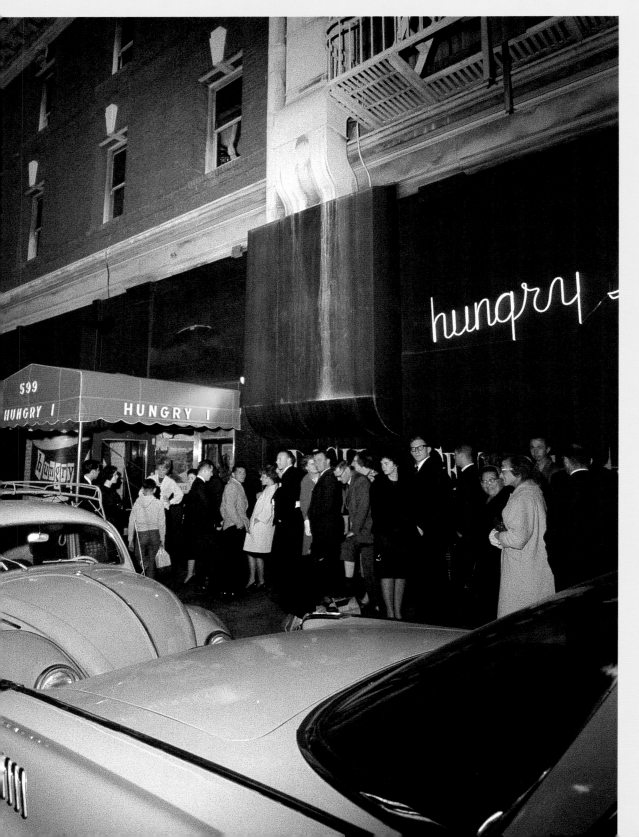

Feisty visionary, bon vivant, and talent scout extraordinaire Enrico Banducci founded the hottest bar-lounge in San Francisco during the '60s. It was called the hungry i. The basement club didn't serve up rock 'n' roll—it was a jazz club filled nightly with international celebrities applauding a playbill of stand-up comics and folk singers. Headliners included Dick Gregory, Mort Sahl, Jonathan Winters, Barbra Streisand, Lenny Bruce, and others. Many on the long list were "discovered" by the energetic Enrico.

Banducci combined music with comedy and hired golden-throated folk singers, including the Limeliters; Peter, Paul and Mary; and the Kingston Trio. One night a teenager from New York opened with her first gig. She did a twenty-minute program, filling in for Woody Allen, who had frozen with stage fright his first night on stage. Her name was Barbra Streisand.

Left: Crowds flocked to the hungry i, a jazz club in San Francisco. Owner Enrico Banducci found new talent who became international celebrities after first appearing at the hungry i.

Right: Dick Gregory was one of the many new talents who performed in this popular North Beach club.

"There will always be comedy because laughter is part of life, and life goes on."

—ENRICO BANDUCCI

The Sexual Freedom League

I stumbled on the Sexual Freedom League at Oakland High School. A young woman was distributing information leaflets about the organization from a card table she had set up in the school's main hallway. When she invited me to one of the SFL's weekend parties, I accepted. The Sexual Freedom League promoted nudity, among other things. Nudity was synonymous with freedom for hippies, and sexual freedom was part of the equation. People had

The Sexual Freedom League promoted nudity, which was seen as synonymous with freedom.

been having sex since time began, they said, and would continue to do so, so it was about time that fact was recognized. The founder, Jeffery Poland, was a swarthy young man from New York who legally changed his name to Jeff "Fuck" Poland. To bring notice to the three-woman one-man organization, he organized nude events at public beaches and private homes, with grand acceptance from Bay Area students. To the delight of the hippies, the establishment considered any sort of nudity unabashed deviant behavior and loudly summoned the police. The Sexual Freedom League succeeded in generating a lot of community outrage. Never mind that the Condor and several other North Beach clubs had topless programs six times a night and weekend amateur co-ed strip shows.

The Sexual Freedom League started the nude beach phenomenon in California at San Gregario Beach, six miles south of San Francisco.

The Condor Club

By comparison to the rest of the city, San Francisco's North Beach is a mix of ethnic groups and nightlife attractions, with a Mediterranean feel—coffeehouses, sidewalk cafes, bookshops, intriguing restaurants, and visitors from around the world. North Beach borders Chinatown by Broadway, a wide avenue starting at the Bay running west through Russian Hill. The part near the Bay, up to Columbus Avenue, was once the infamous Barbary Coast and still markets libidinous temptations.

A thirty-foot, blinking, red-nippled nude figure, the Condor Club sign dominated the northeast corner of Broadway and Columbus. This was the place featuring the hot new action, topless! It soon became topless and bottomless, then virtually inhibitionless entertainment. The Condor Club was run by two dark Italians—a jockey-size Gino del Prete, and his angular partner, Pete Matteoli. They were helped by their rotund PR man, Davy Rosenberg. The 360-pound promoter modestly billed himself as "The World's Greatest Press Agent." Covering the door were a white-suited midget—Villechaize, later to be famous for "da plane! da plane!" on *Fantasy Island*—and Eddy, a 7'3" giant.

It was SRO in Frisco all right. The show at the Condor commenced when a quartet swung into "The Resurrection Roll." Miss Doda waiting in a crawl space, in the ceiling, crouched low on an upraised piano, waiting for the cue. With the clash of a cymbal, the piano started down. In the flickering spotlight, the star—twitching, convulsing, and gyrating to the "swim,"—descended on a white baby grand piano. The other clubs in North Beach immediately followed suit; "Topless" became the favored spectator sport.

Always a city of contrasts, San Francisco is sometimes difficult to fathom. Reluctantly, the city fathers had accepted Ginsberg's *Howl* at the end of the fifties. Yet in 1965, a half block west of the Condor, the police arrested playwright Michael McClure at Allen Meyerson's Committee Theatre for a legitimate theater performance of *The Beard*. Jean Harlow and Billy the Kid, wearing paper beards, aboard a spacecraft, argue over giving and receiving love. Profanity is used, and there is the suggestion of sexual content. The arrest charge: Violation of Section 182, Suspicion of Conspiracy to Commit a Felony. Any sexual suggestion performed in the public view was too much for the guardians of public morals. Ironically, three hundred feet down the block, garnering long lines, was the Condor. Across the street was the Garden of Eden, with its marquee shouting "The Positions of Love" and glossy photographs of a near-nude couple acting out a simulation of sex. Billed as the Love Dance, it was performed on purple velvet cushions five times a night. Yet across town, the San Francisco Mime troop was busted for putting on a free play in a city park without a permit. Those were heady times.

Every day youthful craziness and the establishment's double standard appeared in the newspapers. Reporting the corruption of public morals was making the *San Francisco Chronicle* famous.

The famous Condor Club in North Beach offered "topless" entertainment nightly.

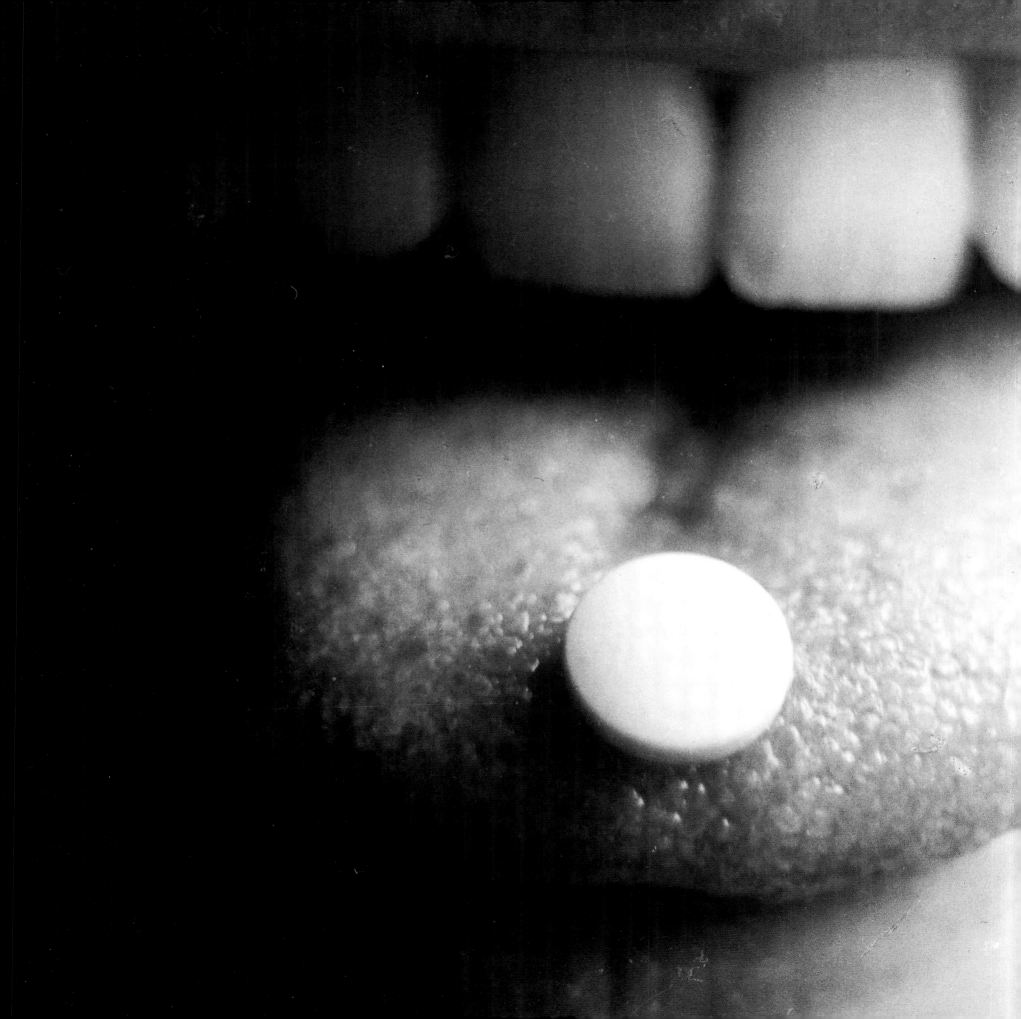

Drugs

By 1965, the Haight-Ashbury was collecting notoriety for weird behavior associated with the new drug LSD. LSD was legal in California until its moratorium on October 6, 1966. It was also the object of my curiosity.

Part of my own enthusiasm for the hippie lifestyle was connected to the drug. Over previous years, I had heard intriguing rumors about mushrooms that could expand consciousness, and Dow Chemical was marketing Better Living Through Chemistry. LSD had been billed as mind-expanding, and that idea touched me. What did it mean? My research, I thought, would make a fascinating story. I had witnessed Yuri Geller's spoon bending at Stanford, which reinforced my belief in the untapped potential of the mind. But little else had been documented outside the sterile, white-coated environment of a research laboratory.

Street LSD was initially produced by an East Bay chemistry wizard, Dr. Augustus Owsley Stanley III. Stories had been circulating about research of LSD at the Palo Alto Veterans Administration Hospital. On the East Coast, two psychology professors at Harvard University, Dr. Timothy Leary and Dr. Richard Alpert, had become leading advocates of the drug, calling it "The most potent hallucinogenic drug known to science," (*Playboy* interview, September 1966). It was colorless, odorless, and tasteless, but an incredibly powerful compound. LSD was first synthesized by Dr. Albert Hofmann, the Swiss biochemist seeking a painkiller for migraine headaches at the Sandoz Laboratory in Switzerland in 1938. Aldous Huxley's *Doors of Perception* discusses his own involvement with the drug and was much quoted in books and journals. Huxley embraced the cause

The sixties saw the advent of LSD, a new mind-expanding drug that would change American culture.

Orange sunshine, blue light, blue cheer, purple haze, clear light, and loading zone were street names for early LSD.

Haight Street. This was prior to October 6, 1966, when California declared LSD illegal. Rock bands used names of acid to identify themselves and their songs.

In the early days a single dose of acid cost two dollars and was taken using a sugar cube as the medium; the drug gave the cubes a pink cast. By 1967, LSD was packed into more controllable "tabs" of 250 micrograms (1 millionth of an ounce)—this gave a trip of 6 to 8 hours. There was also liquid-impregnated blotter paper divided into stamps, facilitating better handling. As one might expect, acid stamps appeared as decorated sheets with images, sometimes depicting the territory at the end of the psychedelic rainbow. Blotter acid stamps were soon a collector's art with Felix the Cat, the Grateful Dead skull, the Egyptian eye, the Giza pyramids, a peace dove, UFOs, a smiley face, images of Tim Leary, the word *pure*, and even my image of the Kesey bus, among others.

One didn't "take a pill." Rather people talked about "eating" acid. With the correct dose, its users fell into "...a remarkable but not unpleasant state of intoxication ...intense stimulation of the imagination and an altered state of awareness of the world," (Hofmann). One afternoon in Golden Gate Park, I watched a young woman examining a handful of dirt for what I considered to be a very long time. When I had to pass on, some minutes later, the woman was still examining the object of her curiosity. It was only later that I would understand.

My first experience with LSD came, inadvertently, at the Trips Festival. It was not a full-blown acid episode, but it had many of the effects—difficulty speaking coherently, vision swaying, and rainbows of color. Some of that was present, yet I managed to take my photographs, and found the floor to be a steady platform. I likened the experience to helm duty in heavy weather at sea, after a few hot whiskey coffees.

Zig-zag papers used to roll marijuana cigarettes.

for hallucinogens, calling his drug experience " . . . without question the most extraordinary and significant experience of my life." This advanced my own curiosity. At the time, the negative effects of LSD experienced by some were still not fully understood.

As each batch of Owsley acid was produced in his Berkeley hills laboratory, it was given an exotic name identifying the brew. Early on, there was Orange Sunshine, Blue Light, Blue Cheer, Purple Haze, Clear Light, Loading Zone, and other names hawked by salespeople on

"I have gone beyond
vision into many of the experiences
described in Eastern and Western
literature — the transcendence of the subject-
object relationship, the sense of solidarity with all
the world so that one actually knows by experience
what 'God is Love' means: the sense that, in spite
of death and suffering, everything is somehow and
ultimately All Right; the sense of boundless gratitude
at being privileged to inhabit this universe. Blake
says, 'Gratitude is heaven itself' — it used to
be an incomprehensible phrase, now I know
precisely what he was talking about."

DOORS OF PERCEPTION,

Aldous Huxley

Left: Marijuana joints were a common sight in the Haight-Ashbury; sharing food and drugs was a common theme with the hippies.
Right: A farmer in Mexico harvests marijuana to be sold in the U.S.
Far right: The pot is weighed before packaging.

Marijuana

Marijuana was the drug of choice among the counter-culture. In the twenties, smoking pot (or "reefer," as it was called) had been the second choice—mainly a cheap high popular in the South with jazz musicians during Prohibition. In the fifties, pot was used by the avant-garde. Poets and writers were smoking marijuana as a new expression of protest against the establishment.

Above: Kilo packages of marijuana sold for $80 in the U.S. One "key" was enough marijuana for a hippie to live on in the Haight-Ashbury. Hippies sold "lids" (a full ounce) for $10.
Right: Two friends share a joint.

Rock 'n' Roll

Touring Swing dance bands, Jazz, Dixieland, Folk, Bebop, and Rhythm and Blues had been the music till Rock was imported from London and touched America. To some degree, that was the music context, starting in the fall of 1965. There was lots of Blues and Jazz around town, but the excitement experienced at the Appeals, up at 1090 Page, and at a few "events" ("A Tribute to Sparkle Plenty" and "A Tribute to Ming the Merciless" produced by Chet Helms and Rock Scully) was circulating rapidly around Bay Area campuses. The primary mode for getting the word out for a rock 'n' roll band was Ralph J. Gleason's *Chronicle* music column. Radio and posters were also essential. The main-stream commercial music was R&B, Bebop, and Folk. San Francisco rock had yet to be recognized as commercially viable until 1967. Some of the great musicians to come out of this San Francisco scene were Jimi Hendrix, Janis Joplin, Grace Slick and the Jefferson Airplane, Jim Morrison, and Jerry Garcia and the Grateful Dead.

Jimi Hendrix and his band rock to the music at the Oakland Auditorium.

The sound and energy of Janis Joplin evoke the magic of the sixties for many fans even today.

Facing and this page: George Harrison and his wife Patti paid a visit to the Haight-Ashbury in June of 1967 to the delight of the hippies, who followed the couple on a walk up and down Haight Street.

Rock icon Jimi Hendrix became immensely popular during the sixties.

Above: Fans and hippies jam the Panhandle for a
free concert by the Grateful Dead.
Right: The Grateful Dead pose for this picture
inside Jerry's room at 710 Ashbury in 1967.

This page and facing: The "Dead," the quintessential band of the sixties, pose in their living room at 710 Ashbury, rehearse at the heliport in Sausalito, and pose with other San Francisco rock bands in front of 710.

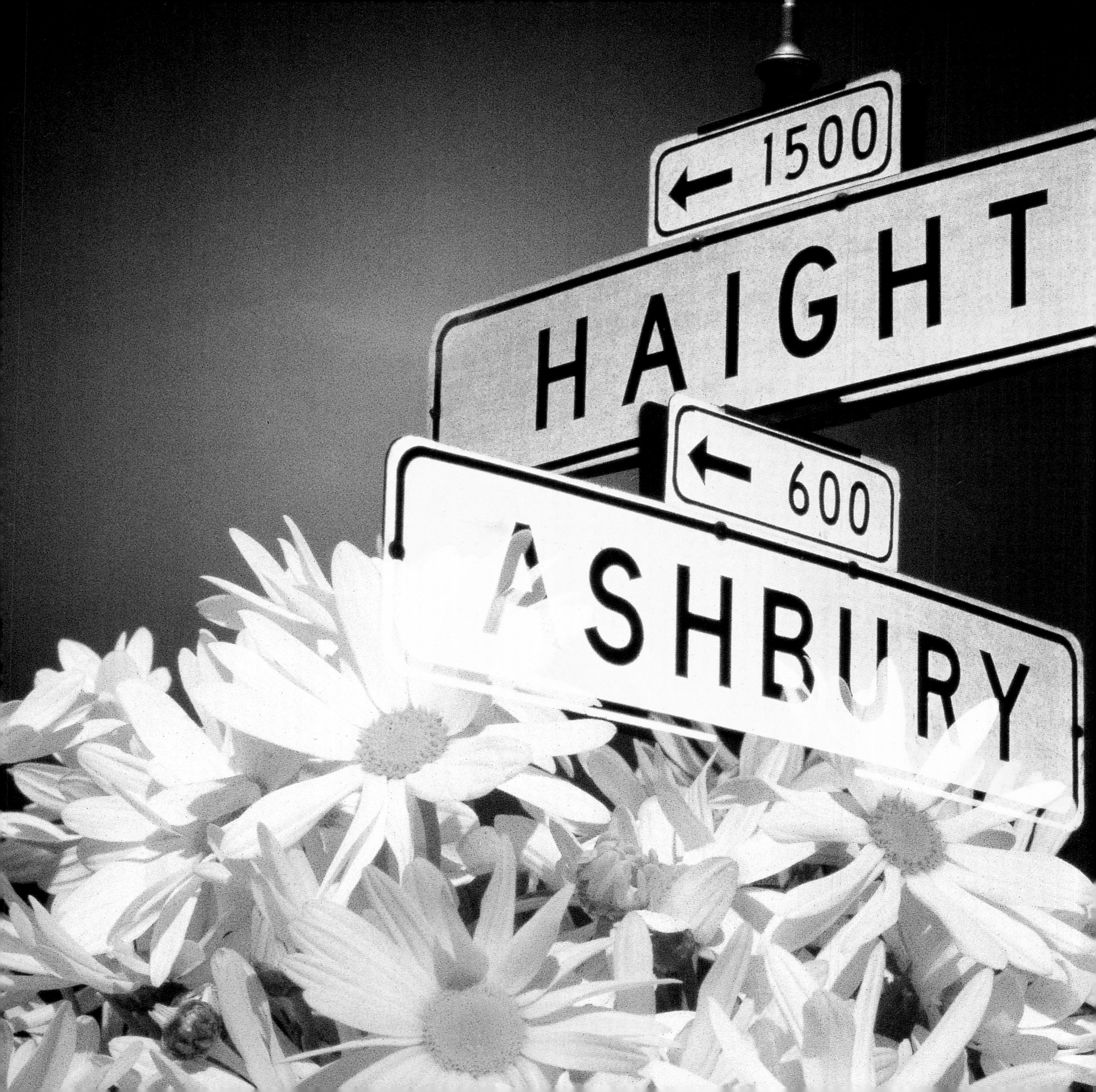

1500
HAIGHT
600
ASHBURY

Family and Tribe

Family and tribe were words often heard in the Haight-Ashbury.
Many young people in the Haight lived communally in the large Victorian buildings. People of like mind-set mingled resources and offered emotional support. This created the sense of family that many were seeking. Young girls and runaways could deal with their needs in a communal atmosphere that was usually creative and meditative, with a background of rock 'n' roll and raga music. Sharing—whether it was food, pot, money, or shelter—was woven into the communal ethic.

Generally quiet, most hippies were well-mannered. Most of the kids appeared to come from middle-class families. Early on, the police were tolerantly amused by the changing lifestyle. In 1966 and '67, young girls stood on Haight Street corners, hawking the new journalism—the *San Francisco Oracle* and the *Berkeley Barb*—and distributing free samples of patchouli oil and the latest LSD tabs, while it was legal.

Each day Haight Street was attracting more kids and their pageantry. It was open house and everybody was invited. There emerged a burgeoning band of jingle-jangling kids, wrapped in blankets or draped with flags, dressed like pirates or cowboys, some playing flutes and horns and bugles. Dogs with flowers tied to their collars ran around the Panhandle. Weekends in the Panhandle offered free concerts, featuring the Grateful Dead, the Jefferson Airplane, the Charlatans, and Big Brother and the Holding Company with Janis Joplin. They played atop flatbed trucks. It was liberation through movement.

Haight-Ashbury was the center of the hippie movement and the summer of love.

From communal living to hanging out on the streets, Haight-Ashbury was home to the flower children.

Street Fashions

Fashions of the hippies were becoming very diverse: freaky, eclectic, homemade, military surplus, Salvation Army, the Edwardian look. Fashions were a window on the new tribe and included leather boots, leather jackets with fringes, long hair, bright colors, beards, and embroidered shirt cuffs and collars lovingly sewn by one's "significant other." Youngsters went barefooted; women wore Levi's. Braless became the style. Silver Indian jewelry, large turquoise belt buckles and rings, necklaces, and wristbands and armbands noting the brotherhood were popular. God's eyes (crossed sticks decorated with colored yarns) warded off evil spirits and decorated many homes and kitchens. Women wore large floppy hats, feathers, black-hooded monk capes, and silky gowns that touched the ground. The Stars and Stripes and the California state flag were popular as clothing. Young women often wore daisies in their hair.

Haight Street was a great spectacle. Les Enfants du Paradis. Costumed street theater. A prevailing presence emerged from the cavernous Victorians around the Haight-Ashbury—drums and laughter, applause, a rhythmic tambourine, strolling musicians, and an odor of patchouli and musk and skunk weed.

Diverse and unusual fashions characterized the hippies. Military surplus, the Edwardian look, top hats, capes, long gowns, leather jackets with fringes, embroidery, and beads were all part of the fun.

Capes, ponchos, and outrageous hats all made a fashion statement. Many in the Haight-Ashbury went barefoot. Both men and women wore long hair, and men wore beards.

Haight Street was always a show. The "action" was about fi ve blocks with the corner of Haight and Ashbury as ground zero. These blocks were the prelude to Golden Gate Park that borders the Haight-Ashbury district.

Drogstore Cafe

Another intersection with unlikely names, Masonic and Haight, was the sight of the Drogstore Cafe. Since the turn of the century this drab two-story building had been a drug emporium. Its new owners kept the décor—the big, brown glass bottles, the glass cabinets—and added their own eclectic touches. The Drogstore Cafe was always loaded, one way or another.

The San Francisco Oracle

The San Francisco Oracle was the psyche-delic, multicolored, perfumed newspaper of the Haight-Ashbury community. It embodied the visual Renaissance and spirit of the counterculture. The *Oracle* included essays about Buddhism and yoga; articles by Allen Ginsberg, Timothy Leary, Gary Snyder, and William Burroughs; articles about the Human Be-In and LSD; poems by Michael McClure and others; commentaries; information; and design. It was the standard and influenced all other underground papers and many established papers and magazines. The *Oracle* has been called the Rosetta stone for future historians who wish to understand the hippie philosophy and creed of an era.

The editor of the paper was Allen Cohen. He had thick, black hair, which he pulled back in a ponytail. Allen tells the story about why he started the paper: "It began with a dream," he says. In his dream, Allen is flying over the tops of people, who are all reading a newspaper with rainbows on it. "A rainbow newspaper!"

Brothers Ron and Jay Thelin, who had opened the Psychedelic Shop on Haight Street in January 1966, helped support the *Oracle*, along with others in the hippie community. Dangerfield Ashton, Michael Bowen, Bruce Conner, Stanley Mouse, Bob Simmons (Azul), and some unknowns contributed art, photography, and copy for its pages. Editorial contributors included Allen Ginsberg, Timothy Leary, Allen Watts, Gary Snyder, Michael McClure, George B. Leonard, and Herman Kahn. For some of the issues, as the papers came off the press, Allen and others sprayed them with patchouli and various other perfumed oils. Printed approximately monthly, the *Oracle* departed from the normal linear newspaper look and created visually exciting space. In 1991, Allen Cohen produced a collection of different editions of the *San Francisco Oracle* in a facsimile edition.

The San Francisco Oracle was the standard for underground newspapers of the counterculture.

Ron and Jay Thelin opened the Psychedelic Shop and helped create the *San Francisco Oracle* at the same time.

Oracle Letter

The *Oracle* and the Psychedelic Shop daily received handfuls of letters from kids all over the country, asking for guidance in their desire to get to the Haight-Ashbury. A young woman in New York poured out her plea:

Dear Oracle people,

This is a plea for help.

I am being held a prisoner. I am the prison that holds me captive and I can't seem to escape myself. Until a few months ago when I saw the Oracle, I thought there was no reason to be alive and was about to settle on merely existing . . . trying to get by the next fifty years or so. But I saw there is more.

But New York can be an awful place. The Lower East Side cannot be believed as to what it does to human dignity and freedom. It seems everyone is looking West.

I am afraid. What if it isn't as it seems? I've heard so much . . . read so much. Your paper is beautiful, beautiful. But because I'm not just stifled by the environment but most of all by myself . . . it is hard to summon the courage to act and come there.

Like anyone, I've been stepped on a lot and have reacted by learning the futility of my words and rarely find the courage to do more than smile at a friendly face.

If I would come, it would be alone. And I would probably never lift my eyes from the sidewalk and how does one make friends or get help if no one can see the plea in your eyes because you are looking down.

The Love Rally here on Easter Sunday was a beautiful thing. All the uptightness in everyone was gone. No need for words . . . people just standing together—loving each other—doing their own thing. No one could believe it was really happening. But for New York the Love Rally ended at sundown.

I know people are trying. The League for Spiritual Discovery is finally open, and there is the Peace Eye Bookstore and a group called the Jade Companions. But they are used by only a select few. I know it's not their fault. I've never been to any of these places other than to walk by and look in hoping for . . . something.

But I am my own prison and I can't escape from myself enough to find what the rally promised there could be here. I know that most of the problems are in my own head. But I also know that I need help. And you are the voice of the place I feel I should be.

If someone has read this far, please, could someone, would someone, take the time to write me and tell me the right things so I won't be afraid to come to San Francisco? Please . . . something concrete—a name, address—something to come to. I need direction and I think maybe I could give a lot if someone would help me . . . or even better, need my help. Thank you. Love, VC, NYC

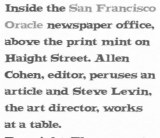

Inside the San Francisco Oracle newspaper office, above the print mint on Haight Street. Allen Cohen, editor, peruses an article and Steve Levin, the art director, works at a table.

Top right: The concept of putting color fountains with black-and-white images was new. The bold page and cover design of the Oracle was revolutionary in the graphics world.

Facing page: A young woman hawks the paper on a street corner.

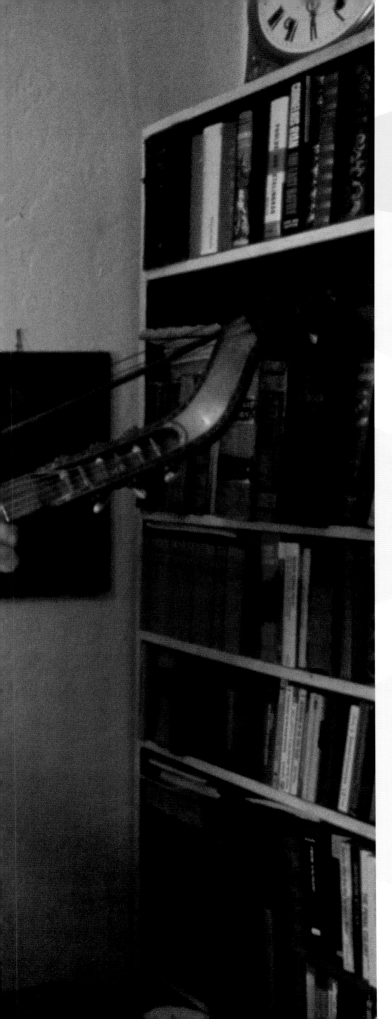

Poster Art

One of the main people associated with the poster art of the sixties was Sätty.

Sätty, spelled with an umlaut over the a, was a poster artist born in Dresden, Germany, and orphaned with a brother after an Allied bomb screamed out of the night sky killing the rest of his family. To address some of his memories, Sätty spent much of his time in pursuit of his art. Tall, with strong Nordic features, he defined himself as "an object in my art." His home in North Beach—which he shared with his wife Martha, a statuesque, blue-eyed woman—was a small museum filled with rich oriental rugs, eighteenth- and nineteenth-century books and antiques, and objects he had picked up during his travels around Europe. His collection overflowed to a storage room, his "secret pad" near the Spaghetti Factory off Grant Avenue in North Beach.

Live Art

Sätty's interest was "live art." He liked to create "little scenes." His art, he said, was externalizing the energy of rock music, ". . . the frenzied action taking place in the ballrooms and in the parks." His poster art was a harmonic, he said, created with the printing press. By passing prints through the press several times he was able to achieve the designs he wanted. Many of his poster images, overprinted on the press, were unique. He also created montage images cut from antique books. I photographed him with other poster artists on the back stairs at the Avalon Ballroom.

Sätty invited me to his "secret pad" to check out "a little scene."

"Sit there and close your eyes until I tell you to open them!" he demanded, pointing to a horsehair-stuffed chair. It was without feet, low on the floor. There was a single overhead light, which he turned off. A moment later there was some movement—someone else came into the room—then Sätty turned on a flickering red-and-yellow lava light that revealed the darkened

Sätty, the poster artist, in his North Beach apartment.
Sätty called himself "an artist within himself."

✳ 111

room. The walls were covered with antique mirrors and objects. The mirrors reflected a young nude woman on a mattress of dark furs and silk pillows. "Eugene," he said, "this is my living scene. Isn't it groovy?"

Sätty's Parties

Sätty loved parties. "Let's party!" he often said spontaneously. Sätty enjoyed parties so much he moved from his second floor flat on Francisco Street, after complaints of gambling, to a ground-floor apartment around the corner on Powell Street. Here he figured out a way to throw great parties under the building, under the floor joists. After descending a ladder positioned over a large hole cut into the floor, guests stepped on thick carpeting taken from the recently demolished Fox Theater on Market Street. The carpet covered a rough dirt surface. To section off the space, he made partitions out of gauzy window curtains. Some areas were so low, people were forced to bend over or sit.

Sätty had provided an assortment of ancient stuffed chairs. He lighted the space with beeswax candles (which helped mask a strong mildew odor), along with antique standing parlor lamps whose shades were made of colored pieces of paper and glass. He also burned incense and sprayed perfume around before a party. The *San Francisco Chronicle* columnist Herb Caen was a regular, attracting the nobs of Nob Hill who trooped down to Sätty's place on a bimonthly summons. His parties were anxiously awaited and shared with artists and photographers. "Eugene, I'm having another party, why don't you drop over after midnight," he would say. Traveling rock bands came by and played all night, shaking the neighborhood around Powell and Francisco Streets. It would drive tourists crazy on the street above, trying to figure out where the sound and vibrations were coming from.

Inside his "secret room" Sätty created objects in living art. Sätty's "underground" parties were literally under the floor joists of a building. He provided stuffed chairs and burned incense. Traveling rock bands played all night long.

The San Francisco Rock Music Posters

As cultural documents, these rock posters refer directly and indirectly to counterculture values. They are a primary graphic record of an idealistic youth movement—a renaissance of spirit, expressed in music, art, and progressive politics.

First, regarding the art itself, these posters expanded the range of graphic expression and perception. Stylistically, unlike conventional posters, these are very decorative, often densely patterned and nonlinear. For this special audience such graphic complexity was most appealing. It was doubly attractive—as an in-group symbol and as an "eye trip." In the process this graphic style established new levels of visual sophistication, of graphic comprehension, and communication.

This do-it-yourself poster industry revived handmade art. Typically, commercial art of the early 1960s consisted of simple typeset block lettering and photography. Rock music posters revived drawing. Their graphic art influenced mainstream commercial art and became an international style. The impetus of this graphic revival extended into the fine air brush illustration of the 1970s and '80s, and on into the computer graphics of the 1990s.

Besides artistic contributions, the posters document personal and cultural values of the psychedelic era. The artists who were participants in the culture were free to express their imagination, as well as their experiences, ideas, personalities, and so on. Made with such artistic liberties, these posters became an expression of the culture, more of a folk art than commercial art. At their best, many of the posters reflect the counterculture's search for liberation, for a new way of being.

Some indication of their documentary value can be

Rock music posters represented the counterculture values. Many had overt political messages.

obtained from a few summaries of the posters' content. These relate to essential aspects of the counterculture, which was both joyous and serious, looking inward and outward in search of self and community.

❈ **Pleasure:** The culture was ebullient, and in content and style some posters evoke high-spirited fun, especially through music and dancing. Others evoke a range of pleasures, from solo mind trips to the sensual and erotic.

❈ **Self-expansion:** A quest for meaning and systems of order was also inherent in the culture. Astrological symbols and other symbols related to religious or philosophical disciplines indicate the intellectual and spiritual desire for understanding, for higher consciousness, and for harmony with the cosmic order.

❈ **Identity and Community:** This maverick psychedelic counterculture, called hippies, established both personal and group identity in part through costume. Rejecting modern aesthetic values, they adopted old-fashioned styles (both plain and elegant), blue-collar work clothing, and sometimes the flashy, quasi-military uniforms of marching bands and similar groups. Long hair for men was popularized by the Beatles, but there were also indigenous models in Western American culture of the nineteenth century for this style, such as the hardy

Above: The do-it-yourself poster industry revived handmade art. Here poster artist Rick Griffin is working on his famous "eyeball" poster. *Right:* Sätty with his poster montage.

mountain men. Most prominent was the Native American, a tragic but noble and revered figure symbolic to hippies of the outsider. Native American images and references are found throughout the poster art, and this folk hero also provided the term commonly used for group identity: the tribe. An early 1966 poster is titled: "A Tribal Stomp," and the January 1967 "Be-In" was promoted as "A Gathering of the Tribes."

—Walter Medeiros 30 April 2003

Diggers

I met sixteen-year-old Phyllis Wilner at the Drogstore Cafe.

She had been sitting with Michael Bowen the first day I ventured into the Haight. Phyllis had read a notice tacked to a bulletin board near the door; the words were set in a design of a falling snowflake: "Free Free Free Food Food Free Food Free. Today at the Panhandle at 4 PM." It offered a place to go, so Phyllis, new in town, asked directions to the Panhandle. It was a few blocks away.

The Diggers showed up at the Panhandle with large army field kitchen kettles filled with soup du jour and boxes of sandwiches made in the basement of The Church of Jesus Christ of Latter-day Saints a block away. Peter Berg, Emmett Grogan, and Peter (Coyote) Cohon (who were initial Diggers) started the Free Store, a garage at 1778 Page Street. Over the entrance, a large, yellow, painted wooden frame leaned against the side of the building. Ten feet high and fifteen feet wide, it was known as the free-frame-of-reference. It was set up in the middle of the street, defining their stage. Since the Mime Troupe was performing without a city permit, their rationale was that law protects art, therefore anything performed "within a frame" was art.

The Free Store was filled with boxes of clothes and other useful and useless items, free for the taking. Everything was free. There was a makeshift tire swing in the middle of the garage where anyone could take a free ride. Asking a Digger a simple question like who was in charge would prompt the response, "You are." In the end, the Diggers initiated a consciousness.

The Diggers contributed a lot of the mystique that was so much a part of the Summer of Love and the Haight-Ashbury. Many of the Diggers were members of the San

Diggers in the Panhandle. It was the image of the Green Beret trooper that caught the author's attention.

Francisco Mime Troupe. As actors and revolutionaries, they were fully engaged in the hippie revolution on many levels within the community. If the Diggers had picked a key word to describe themselves, that word would have been *absurd.* To announce oneself as a Digger was to *be* a Digger: a "heavy" hippie and a one-percenter, as symbolized on the Digger poster. The one-percent symbol was borrowed from the Hell's Angels, another heavy fraternity that also played a role in the Summer of Love. The Hell's Angels wore a shoulder patch on their jackets to proclaim one-percent status as bikers. "Ninety-nine percent of all motorcyclists," says the American Motorcycle Association, "are decent, law-abiding citizens."

Peter Berg, a founding member of the Diggers, told me, "We put the one-percent symbol on our poster because we were saying that one percent of the people were willing to pull out all the stops to help change our society. The symbol was elitist. It was a challenge. It meant 'join us.'"

Above: The Diggers— Sculptor La Mortadella, Emmett Grogan, Slim Minnaux, Peter Berg, and Butcher Brooks—on the steps of City Hall after charges of creating a public nuisance were dropped in court. The Diggers were culprits of street theater to the shock of the local cops who arrested them.
Left and facing page: The Diggers promoted the social ideal of free food and clothing. They often served soup and sandwiches at the Panhandle.

Diggers go far back in history. A large group of people called themselves Diggers in the seventeenth century; they were an anarchistic communal farming group in Cromwellian England. They wanted the land outside of London to be free for all who needed to use it. The hippie philosophy of love and compassion was an ideal that the modern-day Diggers promoted with free food and clothing, and with street theater as a means of communication.

A giant bubble of enthusiasm was spreading around the Bay Area in the mid-1960s. On the other side of the Bay in Berkeley there were mounting pockets of paranoia and greater numbers of people protesting the war in Vietnam. The craziness around the Haight-Ashbury and the growth of rock 'n' roll were like a diversion to the politics. Painters, sculptors, dancers, and other talented artists were enthusiastically pursuing their work in San Francisco. There were also too many young and naive runaway kids, homeless and hungry, trying to find their destiny.

The values of the sixties promoted a sense of connection with others that often resulted in parties, dancing, theater, and personal expression.

Facing: The Hell's Angels came to the Haight-Ashbury to buy LSD.

Below, left: Hell's Angels were rebels incarnate who dressed up to intimidate people.

Above: Headstones of the Hell's Angels in Oakland Cemetery.

Right: Hell's Angel "Chocolate George."

Hell's Angels

The notorious Hell's Angels motorcycle club members (who Ginsberg referred to as the "Angelic Barbarians") were literally invited into the hippie conclave by Mr. Kesey. As a seasoned veteran of LSD, Kesey had been involved with the substance as a $75 per day volunteer guinea pig at the Menlo Park Veterans Hospital in 1961. Kesey and company, including Jerry Garcia, reasoned that it would be interesting to know how the Angels would react with a few doses of Dr. Augustus Owsley Stanley III's elixir. There are some who claim that for a time LSD did have a calming effect on the Angels. After the first meeting between Kesey and the Pranksters, a kind of bond was created between the hippies and the Hell's Angels.

Leading Mr. Behan Astray

The perpetual exuberance and party atmospherics of the hippies were not exclusively confined to youthful bohemians: it also loomed over some of old San Francisco. Keeping the spirit of San Francisco's hospitality alive, one memorable event endeared me to Dublin's prodigal playwright son, Brendan Behan, who declared himself a Digger. Mr. Behan had come to town to assist in the opening of his play Borstal Boy at the Curran Theater. But from the start, owing to Mr. Behan's daily consumption of "the bubbley," his presence at the theater had become an embarrassment. That was all right — Brendan wanted to see the hippies anyway. His guide would be a young hippie lady, who escorted the playwright around town. Unfortunately, a couple of bottles of champagne and some loud soliloquies rendered in the lobby of the very proper Cliff Hotel earned him a night in the slammer. Fortunately he was released the next morning in time to have lunch with one of San Francisco's most esteemed plutocrats — Louis Lurie, who happened to own the Curran Theater. Invited to lunch at Jack's, a vintage restaurant also owned by Mr. Lurie, Brendan showed up not quite ready to be honored, arm in arm with his hippie lady. Especially chagrined were other leading socialites. The hippies were never forgiven for leading Mr. Behan astray.

The Love Pageant Rally in the Panhandle was held to bring attention to the moratorium on LSD, October 6, 1966.

Appeal Parties

When I entered the Haight-Ashbury scene, the San Francisco Mime Troupe

was embroiled in a legal matter with the city's Recreation and Park Department over the issue of the Mime Troupe holding free performances in the city parks. The Mime Troupe's production of *Il Candelaio,* a sixteenth-century farce, was deemed "not in good taste, and illegal without a permit." The matter went to court, and to raise expenses, Bill Graham created a benefit flier announcing the San Francisco Mime Troupe's "Appeal Party."

My first contact with Bill Graham was in the fall of 1965, at a street parade in the city's financial district where he was helping promote the first San Francisco Mime Troupe "Appeal." Bill was with a group of people—a small parade that included a couple of open vintage cars, honking for attention in the slow noon-hour traffic moving down Montgomery Street. The cars were draped with bed sheets and painted with black-and-red letters: "S. F. Mime Troupe party!" Mime Troupe people were running alongside the cars handing out fliers and slowing traffic. The fliers announced "Appeal I," a benefit to be held the next night, a Friday, for the Mime Troupe at their headquarters, known as "the Loft," near the *Chronicle* building. Two weeks earlier the media had covered the Mime Troupe bust, and as a follow-up story covered the Appeal parade down Montgomery Street. That night Graham's bit of street theater got on the evening news. Once again the media became a free vehicle to augment the counterculture circuit.

The San Francisco Mime Troupe held Appeal Parties to support their right to hold free performances in San Francisco parks.

Born Wolfgang Grajonea, Bill Graham had a singleness of purpose, vision, and spirit that were elements he offered to the Summer of Love. Bill was my initial contact with the unfolding scene, and in retrospect, his life

exemplifies the philosophy and alchemy for rending straw into gold. It was fall 1965, and Bill Graham was about to participate, in a significant way, in the launching of San Francisco's rock 'n' roll scene.

Bill was an orphan and refugee of the Holocaust. He used to say, "I remember going into water-filled trenches once the bombing raids started . . . I was terrified." He also said, "Home to me wasn't my family. Home to me was all those other kids. I was part of something. It was my base, it was my home."

In 1955, Bill was granted a name change, then drafted into the army, where he earned a combat Bronze Star in Korea. Discharged, Bill worked as a waiter, a "Mountain Rat," in the old Jewish family mountain resorts in the Adirondacks, where some of the dining rooms could accommodate four thousand guests at a seating. He later found his way to San Francisco and took a job as business manager for the San Francisco Mime Troupe.

Above: Bill Graham had a huge role in the entertainment scene of the sixties, from organizing Appeal Parties to managing the Fillmore.
Right: Holding his bank book in his hand, Bill Graham has just learned that after weeks of controversy the city has granted him a dance hall permit for the Fillmore.

The Appeal Party Flier

Written by Bill Graham, the San Francisco Mime Troupe "Appeal" party handbill shows us another side of Bill Graham's character and motivation. Freedom to create one's own agenda was a basic tenet of the emerging counterculture, and Appeal I was all about freedom and Bill's intolerance for its abuse. The demise of his mother and two sisters, victims of the holocaust, played a strong role in Bill's mindset.

> "R. G. Davis, director of the San Francisco Mime Troupe, was found guilty on November 1 of performing in the public parks without a permit. The four-day trial was pointless because the court did not allow the only relevant issue, freedom of speech and assembly, to be considered. The Park Commissioner judged the Mime Troupe's production in the park 'not in good taste.'
>
> "The trial settled nothing. The Mime Troupe is determined to fight until the parks are returned to their only 'owners,' the people of San Francisco. For this is what it is all about: who owns the parks?
>
> "S. F. Mime Troupe 'Appeal' Party—Saturday night—November 6, from 8 PM to dawn. Entertainment, Music, Refreshments! Engagement, Commitment & Fresh Air!"

The Appeals

The Appeals were patterned after Kesey's Acid Tests and the Sunday night family skit parties in the Adirondacks. The Appeals were jammed with hundred of students and older folks, all frolicking, some dancing by themselves (a new phenomena), or just hanging out, sitting on the floors or on old beat-up couches and stuffed chairs. Many partygoers wore elaborate homemade gowns and masks; others wore cowboy and Indian outfits. The Jefferson Airplane played while colored lights and film loops were projected on walls hung with bed sheets. Pieces of string, suspended from the rafters, held Christmas ornaments and penny candy.

The Appeals and Acid Tests were an important milestone for people of the Bay Area and the Summer of Love. Few people had ever witnessed such a spectacle and enthusiastically told their friends. The year of 1965 finished with two more Appeals for the Mime Troupe and another Kesey Acid Test. The last Acid Test was at the Fillmore before the Trips Festival. The Trips Festival was to be held at the Longshoreman's Union Hall and would combine all the events.

The Appeal Benefit was held in a warehouse, an old, two-story building on Howard Street known as the Calliope Warehouse. Once a hay storage loft, it was constructed with heavy wooden beam floors and beam ceilings. The warehouse space was sectioned off, and one area served as headquarters for the San Francisco Mime Troupe. Other parts of the building were rented out. One tenant was the new rock band, the Jefferson Airplane. Bill Graham's baptism into show business and the beginning of his career in "audience assemblage," as he called it, began with that first Appeal, Saturday, November 6, 1965.

Politics of 1966

The New Year of 1966 arrived with President Johnson firmly at the helm of state. *Time Magazine* was reporting that Johnson was the overwhelming choice of Americans as the "Most Admired Man" in the world. He made serious-faced speeches about his "sincere efforts" in new talks with North Vietnam, offering "peace in our time." He said he was "giving added urgency and sincerity" to his offer of unconditional negotiations with a "Peace Offensive," all the while continuing B-29 carpet bombing raids on the North Vietnamese. Newspapers were disclosing new escalating totals for U.S. military manpower at 190,000. "Until peace comes," said the president, "or if it does not come, our course is clear. The days may become months, and the months may become years, but we will stay the course as long as aggression commands us to battle." As arduous as his job was, President Johnson's greatest contribution is likely his signing of the Civil Rights legislation.

The San Francisco Mime Troupe was part of the sixties scene.

Happenings

The audience as art had been the secret ingredient for success at Kesey's Acid Tests, growing out of "Happenings" first conceived by Gerd Stern and Steve Durkee in 1960. Allen Ginsberg was also a participant with the "Happening" shows that Stern and Durkee developed and produced at San Francisco State.

Gerd, a part-time public relations man when I first met him, figured that if the audience participated in the programs, their alliance would render an event a greater success. Steve, a painter who was living in upstate New York, created hologram images that were later used in their programs. Kesey built on the "Happening" concept to create what he called Acid Tests. Bill Graham built on the Acid Tests to create the success of the Appeals.

Bill Graham's genius was in recognizing and molding individual elements. The simple act of having the audience pass a large beach ball around created a synergy that was enhanced by additional elements like strobe lights, liquid light shows, and rock 'n' roll. Adding to that, people were asked to come wearing costumes. "Audience dancing is an assumed part of all the shows; you are invited to wear ecstatic dress and bring gadgets and toys. AC outlets will be provided."

The Dog House

As a child of six, Chet Helms assisted his grandfather, a Baptist minister, in setting up churches around his hometown, Austin, Texas. Chet's Tuesday night jam sessions at 1090 Page in the Haight were the bridge to the Avalon Ballroom. Ten-Ninety, as the house became known, was where Chet started Big Brother and the Holding Company, and brought Janis Joplin to San Francisco from Austin.

Early on, Chet managed a rooming house on Pine Street where each of the tenants owned a dog. It was known as the Dog House. For a while, some of the roomers were going to go into a dog cemetery business that they would call The Family Dog. The pet cemetery scheme didn't work out, but the name was too good for Chet to ignore. Soon enough, Chet's Pine Street management ended and he moved to 1090 Page, a Victorian mansion in the Haight. It was kismet, destiny, or fate, but 1090 had a basement ballroom complete with a small stage, where Chet produced fifty-cent Saturday night jam sessions. His band depended on the talents of four roommate rock 'n' rollers. Chet became the group's manager. Drawing up a long list of possible names for the new band, the group decided on the last two names: Big Brother and the Holding Company. Chet was the most visible, as the producer of rock 'n' roll programs at various venues around the city. By 1966, he opened the Avalon Ballroom, at Van Ness and Sutter, a walk-up, second-floor dance hall that competed with Bill Graham's Fillmore, which was twelve blocks west, at Geary and Fillmore Streets. Chet had a small office, The Family Dog, on Offarel Street, a few blocks west, where he held court during the day. He could also be found most nights at the head of the stairs of the Avalon. Chet also stood out,

Kids surround the "goodie bar" at the Avalon Ballroom, presided over by Mr. and Mrs. Zaidlin.

physically, because he possessed a handsome golden mane that hung to his waist.

Chet described that era in these words:

"I was a political activist, a lefty, got involved with the Civil Rights Movement in Texas. Got involved with the SDA, Students for Direct Action. I was an ass kicker. That organization became SDS. Students for a Democratic Society. It was organized at the University of Texas, a certain cabal of mostly Jewish graduate students from the East Coast or the Midwest like Chicago. I came to realize that most confrontational demonstrations were fruitless, in most situations...they got attention but it was a negative

Chet Helms ran the "Family Dog" that started out as a dope enterprise then turned to management of rock groups including Big Brother and the Holding Company.

> "The American businessman dreams of romantic fantasies, and they remain fantasies. As far as I am concerned, there is a certain honesty in living out your fantasies." —CHET HELMS

attention. The problem was to get positive programming messages into any kind of mainstream media. The Beatles came along and showed us how to get that attention. But the Beatles borrowed it from the twenties black music ...from 'mama's got a squeeze box, gonna squeeze it all night long!' I was trying to put together a message band, with a model of the Beatles. There were only a few people trying to do it at the time. It really wasn't more than a 'squeckel band,' people beating on a Quaker Oats box. The Blue Yard Hill band. At that time I was kind of homeless. I was a couch surfer. 'Ten-Ninety,' a Victorian mansion on Page Street, had its own ballroom that could accommodate a crowd of two hundred people. It was a boarding house with Art Academy and State College students. We had these Tuesday Night Jam Sessions. One of the roomers was Peter Albin, whose family had a connection to the old house. We didn't have any admission charge because the audience was mainly friends and wives and their friends. Then, to thin out the crowd, we started charging 50 cents. The charge was to get some control because we started to have a lot of underage drinking and pot smoking. This was an era when one could go to prison for a single roach. Bruce Conners, who was a friend of Peter Albin, presented one of the early light shows there. He brought a lot of short films that he had made that were largely stock footage that had a lot of quick cuts. So we showed the films with the jam sessions. At that time there was a real dearth of live music, people danced to records.

"I wasn't into the shows as a business to make money. I thought of it as a Cultural Revolution, as a mission: I was a missionary. I was brought up to be an evangelist. My grandfather was a Baptist minister, and I learned a lot about stagecraft as a kid just watching my grandfather put churches together. My uncles were printers who printed newspapers and biblical tracks."

When Chet was asked about the hippie work ethic, he responded by saying that there was a wide difference between individuals. "So much of work as we have known it to be in America is 'make work.' We are producing too many things nobody needs, and spending labor on items which could be manufactured with less effort by use of more efficient technology. Hippies are willing to work, and some like myself work sixteen hours a day, but they are reluctant to devote forty hours a week to tasks which are boring—if they also happen to be unnecessary."

He continued: "Most hippies are reacting to the experiences of seeing their parents made into shells of human beings by demands of the contemporary 'rat race.' The hippies have witnessed talented parents' shackled to roles and to jobs that waste their creative energies. So the kids have resolved not to let this happen to them."

"Hippies tend to live for the moment. The richness of life is living in communication, and communication is of the moment." —CHET HELMS

Trips Festival

Jerry Mander, a protégé of Howard Gossage, a much-celebrated San Francisco advertising man, called me about an interesting meeting he was about to have and invited me over. That was when I met Stewart Brand, Tony Martin, Ramon Sender, and Zack Stewart. They, along with Bill Graham, were discussing a Trips Festival. They wanted to put Kesey's Acid Test event into the Longshoreman's Hall and would incorporate the new elements few people had yet experienced. Bill Graham had been brought in because of his success producing San Francisco Mime Troupe Appeals. By then Bill had produced three Appeals for the Mime Troupe to fight the city over the transgression of street theater without a license. Bill, who wore suits and ties, had a reputation as the "business guy." His expertise for generating ticket marketing was a golden key to success. Jerry's press release was sent out and was received with considerable bewilderment.

Until the Trips Festival, most dance concert events had a box office of a few hundred people that danced to records. Shows that required more space with live musicians were rare, because sound became homogenized. When sound amplifiers were cranked up to acceptable decibel levels in most venues, the sound became distorted, bouncing off walls with echoes and feedback. Sound, inside the poured cement construction of the Longshoreman's Hall, presented just such a dilemma. That was when Ken Babbs stepped in. He was Kesey's friend and an ex-marine Vietnam veteran helicopter pilot. He was also a sound engineer.

The Trips Festival was an innovation in live music, public dance parties. It was a frenzied, throbbing, electronic free-for-all that lasted for three days and never stopped accelerating.

The competition, around town, for the Trips Festival that weekend was B.B. King, James Brown, Errol Garner, Big Mama Thorton, Bola Sete, the Jefferson Airplane, and the Charlatans.

On the day before the Trips Festival, Kesey had promised

Press Release

"Trips Festival—On the weekend of January 21, 22, 23, there will be a giant 'Trips Festival' at the Longshoreman's Hall, which will include just about every possible light-sound trip available. Ken Kesey's group, including his 'Psychedelic Symphony' will take part. There will be two shows nightly, 8 and 12 o'clock.

"The first program, January 21, has Ben Jacopetti of the Open Theater as M. C. and includes some standards from the Open Theater repertoire such as The Jazz Mice, Beatle Readings, The Endless Explosion, The God Box, the Congress of Wonders and other wonders. Stewart Brand's 'America Needs Indians'—'Sensorium 9' with slides and movies about innumerable Indian tribes plus sound tracks, rock 'n' roll, and an eagle bone whistle shares the evening.

"Kesey will M. C. on the Saturday program. There will be 'Parades and Changes' by members of the Tape Music Center and the Dancer's Workshop, the Holding Company rock 'n' roll group will play: there will be a sound-light console and overhead projections and 50 flashlights! Kesey's 'Acid Test' with The Grateful Dead rock group, Ron-Boise and his Electric Thunder sculpture, Hell's Angels, Allen Ginsberg, and an event called 'Neal Cassady vs. Ann Murphy Vaudeville.'

"The third evening is unplanned and the audience is invited to wear 'ecstatic dress' and to bring its own toys. Someone or something called 'Pinball Machine' will M. C. the Open Theater, the Tape Music Center, America Needs Indians, The Dancer's Workshop, Kesey's Merry Pranksters, Vortex, Marshall MacLuhan, and 'the Stroboscopic Trampoline' will take part.

"The stated objective of the series is 'an audience-experience psychedelic reaction without the use of drugs, or how to go up without taking off.'"

The Trips Festival weekend turned out to be the weekend that would change the rock 'n' roll scene forever. It was the start of what would become Raves in the next millennium.

The Trips Festival included every possible light-sound trip available.

Partygoers danced and rocked to the music for three nights.

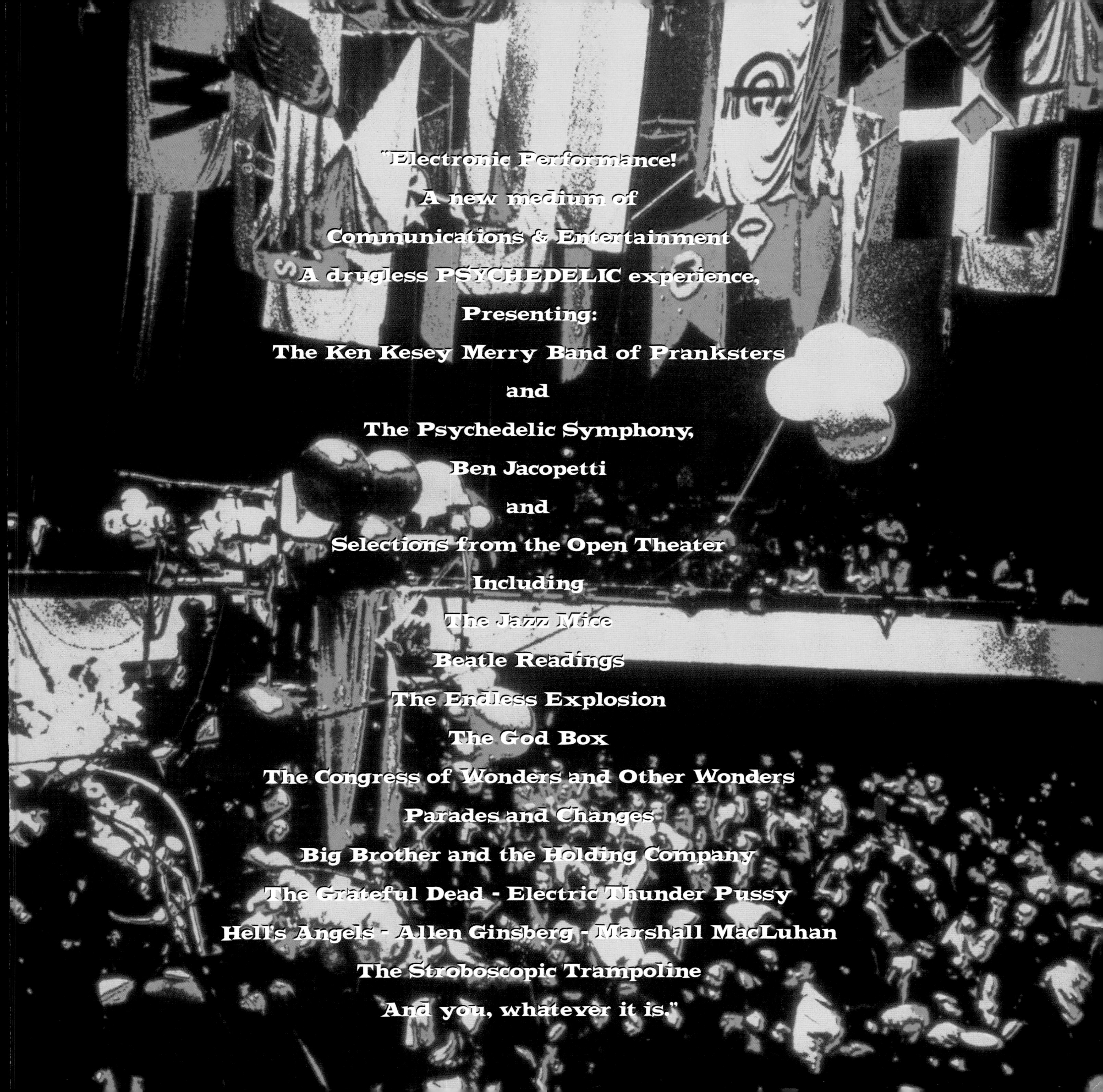

"Electronic Performance!

A new medium of

Communications & Entertainment

A drugless PSYCHEDELIC experience,

Presenting:

The Ken Kesey Merry Band of Pranksters

and

The Psychedelic Symphony,

Ben Jacopetti

and

Selections from the Open Theater

Including

The Jazz Mice

Beatle Readings

The Endless Explosion

The God Box

The Congress of Wonders and Other Wonders

Parades and Changes

Big Brother and the Holding Company

The Grateful Dead - Electric Thunder Pussy

Hell's Angels - Allen Ginsberg - Marshall MacLuhan

The Stroboscopic Trampoline

And you, whatever it is."

From Tom Wolfe's narrative on the Trips Festival from his book The Electric Kool-Aid Acid Test

"An LSD experience without LSD"—that was a laugh. In fact, the heads are pouring in by the hundreds, bombed out of their gourds, hundreds of heads coming out into the absolute open for the first time. It is like the time the Pranksters went to the Beatles concert in full costume, looking so bizarre and so totally smashed that no one could believe they were. Nobody would risk it in public like this. Well, the kids are just having an LSD experience without LSD, that's all, and this is what it looks like. A hulking crazed whirlpool. That's nice. Lights and movies sweeping around the hall, five movie projectors going and god knows how many light machines, interferometrics, the intergalactic science-fiction seas all over the walls, loudspeakers studding the hall all the way around like flaming chandeliers, strobes exploding, black lights with Day-Glo objects under them and Day-Glo paint to play with, street lights at every entrance flashing red and yellow, two bands and a troop of weird girls in leotards leaping around the edges blowing dog whistles—and the Pranksters. Paul Foster has wrapped black friction tape all around his shoes and up over his ankles and swaddled his legs and hips and torso in it up to his rib cage, where begins a white shirt and then white bandages all over his face and skull and just a slit for his eyes, over which he wears dark glasses. He also wears a crutch and sign saying, 'You're in the Pepsi Generation and I'm a pimply freak!' Rotor! Also heads from all over, in serapes and mandala beacs and Indian headbands and Indian beads, the great era for all that. Mojo! Oh the freaking strobes turning every brain stem into a cauliflower erupting into corrugated Ping-Pong balls—can't stand it. Thousands of straight intellectuals and culturati and square hippies, North Beach style, gawking and learning. Dr. Francis Rignew, psychiatrist to the Beat Generation, looking on, all the Big Daddies left over from the Beat period, Eric 'Big Daddy' Nord and Tom 'Big Daddy' Donahue, and the press, vibrating under Ron Boise's thunder machine. A great rout is in progress, you understand."

a judge that he would not associate with any more bad influences, but that night he managed to get busted again, smoking the evil weed with Mountain Girl on a North Beach rooftop.

The Trips Festival was the frenzied, shrieking, throbbing, drum-busting, electronic free-for-all that it had been billed to be. A whirlpool of dancing arm-in-arm to a delirium of light projections, films, and rock 'n' roll. Weird and garish lighting arrangements that had never been seen before thrilled the crowd. It was the mother of all dance concerts and will be remembered as a three-day party that never stopped accelerating.

Many of the elements of that weekend were copied and used from then on, when Bill Graham's Fillmore and Chet Helm's Avalon Ballroom became realities. The Trips Festival became the model with all the theatrics after that, bringing together the eclectic components that Kesey had energized. Organized craziness became a new dimension of show business that burst on the American consciousness.

The Trips Festival was billed as a new medium of

communication and entertainment. California hippies were only half-serious when they described the Trips Festival as a drugless rehearsal for the New Prohibition drug crackdown debate that was gaining attention across the country. LSD had yet to be covered by any legislative controls.

On the last night of the festival people continued to line up at the hall entrance trying to get in. The enthusiasm and hilarity hadn't diminished; it had only expanded from the first night. Older folks, including members of the press, still hadn't figured out what was going on.

The Trips Festival broke new ground in public "assemblage," as Bill Graham liked to call it. The magic came from exploiting the synchronicity of the times, capturing the passion of the moment, and harvesting the creative bubble that was now turning into an alchemy stew. It was an adaptation of the emerging technology, incorporating the latest electronic bells and whistles, with a little help from the Salvation Army, Army Navy Surplus, and rock 'n' roll. It was all new, and as an expression of the times said, "It was a mind blower!"

Below: Light show equipment included overhead projectors with dishes of color dyes and movie projectors that showed bits and pieces of old film— all shown at the same time.
Right: Performers at the Fillmore.

From Ralph Gleason's *Chronicle* review of the Trips Festival, January 24, 1966

Bill Graham's Fillmore Auditorium was a twenties dance hall in the Fillmore district, largely a black neighborhood that had a few jazz clubs. For holidays and special occasions Graham moved his show a few blocks north to the larger Winterland Auditorium that accommodated ice shows and the circus. Graham's penchant for extravaganza began when he held his first New Year's Eve 1967 at Winterland. The midnight tolling included all the cheering and bands playing and the balloons, but when a loincloth-costumed figure emerged in the crowd, captured by a spotlight, riding bare back on a large white steed, freeing white doves, the audience roared its approval and a tradition was born. After the 1967/68 New Year's Party that included Janis Joplin and Grace Slick singing together with the Airplane.

Light Shows

Bill Ham, a light show artist, got the rumor mill in gear when he started projecting his army surplus overhead projectors onto nude dancers in an empty lot across the street, stringing electrical cords from his home on Pine Street. Others had tried 8 mm visual effects with film loops, but Bill, who managed two rooming houses at 1836 and 2111 Pine Street, was first to use the large and powerful army surplus field-projection equipment to project liquid color images as a way to achieve his psychedelic imagery.

A few artists were using 8 mm film loops and projecting 35 mm slide images onto white sheets. Ham put transparent dishes, partially filled with water and colored oils, on top of the overhead projectors. By rotating and tapping the dish to the rhythm of the music, he created rhythmic patterns on his screens. Two weeks following the Trips Festival, Bill Graham opened the Fillmore with the Jefferson Airplane, and the "Sights and Sounds of the Trips Festival."

Before long, Bill Ham was holding informal light show performances for his tenants and neighbors in a basement room. He was later hired by Chet Helms at the Avalon, and in other venues. LSD influenced many artists and designers who tried to present a visual interpretation of hallucinations, through light shows and other arts. Sadly, light shows became wallpaper for the music, and light show art was never fully recognized for its creative dimension.

Light shows were rediscovered in the sixties. The programs depicted the LSD experience for many people.

History of Light Shows

Light shows date back to the 1500s in recorded history, but really began with seafaring. Being a sailor, I knew about spermaceti candles, the first light shows. Spermaceti, or whale grease, could be fashioned into candles for sailors at sea. It was also a valuable base for making perfume and candles for lovers—the hot candles spit colorful sparks, creating an intimate fireworks display. During the coronation of Elizabeth I, the English went all out to create a grand spectacle, and light show art came into its own.

Two glass blowers, Clide Hopper and Jeffery Swallow, recognized that intense light plus transparent color created marvelous visions. A new art form was born. The inventors produced "dissolving views" with two lanterns that projected convergent images, creating three-dimensional moving patterns. The inventors called it "phantasmagoria."

The dissolving views and psychedelic colors of the light shows captured the aura of the sixties drug culture.

Fillmore

Bill Graham produced shows at the Fillmore from December 10, 1965, to July 4, 1968.

It wasn't long before the power elite at San Francisco Northern Police Station (responsible for the Fillmore district) became angry with Graham for his lack of deference and the extra work his enterprise presented. So they applied pressure to shut the Fillmore Auditorium down. Graham was operating with a borrowed dance hall permit, and to stay in business he needed his own. But when Bill applied for a permit he discovered that the police had circulated a petition to the Fillmore neighbors to deny it. The police, however, didn't take into account Bill's tenacity to fight back. He immediately went on the offensive, lobbying friends, politicians, and his Fillmore neighbors.

Chief of Police Tom Cahill seemed to have overlooked San Francisco's long tradition of the public's acceptance and reward for innovation, and continued to fight against the Fillmore. Even letters and pleas from local merchants and neighbors sent to the police didn't cut any favor. Finally, in the end, the *San Francisco Chronicle,* after its own investigation of Bill's situation, supported Graham and the Fillmore Auditorium with an editorial, printed the morning the Board of Permits voted on Graham's petition.

The following night the cops again rolled up a couple of paddy wagons to the front of the Fillmore and arrested fourteen students for being under eighteen years old and in attendance at a public dance. The following morning the *Chronicle* headline read: "Cops Bust Kids for Dancing." Bill was also arrested for a violation, which stated "it is unlawful for a proprietor of a dance hall to admit a minor." But the politicians at City

The Fillmore Auditorium was an institution in the San Francisco area.

Hall quickly realized the error of their ways and gave Bill his dance hall permit. I was in Bill's office when the decision by the Board of Permits granting his dance hall permit was announced on the radio. As Bill listened, a newscaster was breaking the news.

Bill was elated by receiving the permit. He told me that he was following his vision. It was very clear, he said. From his earliest days in San Francisco while helping Ron Davis keep the San Francisco Mime Troupe afloat, Bill had used his basic intuitive knowledge about business. That knowledge had been sharpened by his Mountain Rat days and his afflictive childhood. His past kept him focused. From my perspective he took full advantage of every opportunity with an enthusiasm and energy that was fascinating to observe.

Early one weekend morning after a long night at the Fillmore, I talked with Bill about his passion and work ethic at his favorite after-hours hangout, Mel's Drive-In out on Geary Street. "We run our shows, and we are your peers," he said. "You come to the show, and you have a good time, that's fine. And we won't have a problem. You

The Fillmore Case

"The police department and the Board of Permit Appeals have displayed a misdirected and highly unfair malevolence toward the innocent and highly popular entertainment now being presented at the Fillmore Auditorium.

"With a newly acquired three-year lease, Bill Graham—appraised by *Chronicle* critic John L. Wassermann as 'the best entrepreneur of public entertainment in San Francisco'—has set out to make it the home of assorted productions, ranging from poetry-readings and art shows to rock-and-roll dance concerts. In this last endeavor he is meeting trouble. The police have denied him a dance-hall permit—which previous lessees readily obtained—and the Board of Permit Appeals has declined to overrule the denial.

"This official hostility is not satisfactorily explained. Police say that dance halls attract disorderly crowds and generate fights—but have reported none at the Fillmore Auditorium since Graham took over. Its fire escapes have been called unsafe, but Graham has promptly remedied their defects. Neighborhood opposition has been cited, but Graham has written expressions of goodwill from neighboring churchmen and merchants.

"One suspects that bureaucratic fear, prejudice and instinct for censorship are operating here as they have in somewhat similar situations in the past. This suspicion is strengthened by the testimony of numerous witnesses who have viewed the weekend proceedings at the Fillmore Auditorium and found them interesting, exciting and completely orderly and harmless. They report that participants in the revels—at $2.50 a head—are peaceful and well-behaved though they have long hair, and some wear beards, and few adhere to fashions approved by *Esquire, Vogue,* or the *Gentleman Tailor.*

"The music played by top-quality bands of the genre is loud enough to rattle the windows but it inspires the dancers to remarkable contortions in their free-form versions of the modern dance. Some take the floor as singles and some as duets, but not as partners, for boy seldom meets girl after the gyrating starts.

"It is not disputed that the dancing is chaste and sexless, that the dancers are peaceful and happy, that there are no drunks (only soft drinks and apples being vended on the premises) and that a good time is had by all. The police, formerly sought by Graham to list their objections, have failed to respond and it must seem that they have no case against him. On advice of counsel, he proposed to conduct business at the old stand pending a new appeal—fortified by written testimonials and best wishes from all segments of the Fillmore community. Further refusal of his dance-hall permit cannot be justified in the absolute absence of cause."

earn your dollar and want to spend it right. So you come to the Fillmore."

Bill was generally in motion and talked using his arms and hands to emphasize his meaning. He talked about his ideas for creating a good show, calling it "the dish," and "putting the parsley on the plate."

"Behind the scenes is like the action in a kitchen at any good restaurant," he said. "In the kitchen the cook fights with the waiter, the waiter fights with the dishwasher, and the waiters fight each other, but when they walk through those swinging doors everything clicks." Bill snaps his fingers: One! Two! Three!

"You never show the audience the difficulties. When I was a waiter, I would ask the customer for the order, and he would ask for a piece of lobster. The customer doesn't want to hear the bullshit you had to go through to achieve that dish. The same for my customers. The fans don't want to hear what I had to go through to get the music.

"In between the shows we start tossing a volleyball around, right? It's nice and simple. It moves back and forth, a lot of people move the ball over their heads, pretty soon everyone is entertaining themselves till the real show comes on. It adds something. Just like a clean bathroom adds something to the Fillmore.

"A lot of people come to hear the Grateful Dead not only to be entertained. The audience might not speak to one another, but they will move and rub up against one another, they'll smile or dance with someone they don't know. That just doesn't happen at most shows. You never

The Fillmore was the place to dance, meet friends, or just hang out.

Jim Marshall

Jim Marshall is a photographer known for following much of the sixties music scene. He often had a difference of opinion with Bill Graham, who was notorious for his ability to establish his point. In a closed office, Jim could actually yell louder than Bill. Bill only had respect for people if they had respect for themselves. So Bill and Jim would go at it.

Jim, a man with dark features, piercing dark eyes, and an aquiline nose, concentrated his photography on musicians. My interests as influenced by Dorothea Lange were fixed on the context of the scene, the emotion of the moment. What musicians were wearing, and their sense of style, caught my eye.

In some ways Jim and Bill had similar personalities—sometimes arrogant, and not very forgiving. Jim recognized Bill's roar as louder than his bite. They could certainly scream at each other over a dispute; it would grow with intensity and horrify anyone within earshot. But in the end they seemed to enjoy a good rant and rave.

see a freak-out at the Fillmore; what remains is a wonderful feeling that people are in a familiar surrounding. People are saying "time-out" for the few hours they come to the Fillmore.

"I was raised in New York, and as I grew up, I knew that I basically mistrusted people until I had grounds to trust them. Here on the West Coast when I met people, I gradually got to a point where I trusted people until I had grounds to distrust them. When I'm in New York I'm much more at attention; who are you? What's your position relative to my position, what's your objective? In San Francisco I have a lot more trust. I can get into a cab and relax. In New York I'll check out the cab driver a lot more closely, the waiter, the guy in the elevator. I have a lot more trust out here. The survival ratio on the East Coast is a lot tougher. It's a harder world and much more competitive.

Above: Pranksters Lee Quanstrom and Space Daisey get married at the Fillmore to the delight of friends. Bill Graham provided a wedding cake and the hall, all for free. Below: Friends celebrate at the wedding.

You have to have much more street savvy. You can get away with being more aloof, it's good to be conscious of the space that you're occupying, but somehow man doesn't look to beat you out here as readily as he does back East.

"When I take your ticket what happens to you? I'm concerned about you the way I am about myself, when I go into a theater or a restaurant, I want to be treated decently. Sometimes I make mistakes, things get fouled up, but there is an attempt to treat you the way I would want to be treated.

"I socialize with very few musicians. I have very strong feelings about the shows. The ticket says 8 o'clock, the show starts at 8 o'clock. The bands play two 45 minute sets, they are ready, the equipment is tuned, they're fresh, but a lot of musicians don't exactly feel the same way that I do. So I yell a lot."

I found Bill Graham to be all business, and direct about what he wanted. He was very focused, and most people would abide by his agenda. But he always had time to acknowledge his friends.

Lenny Bruce

Lenny Bruce was a comedian who talked about poverty and starvation and racial issues and made a lot of people angry, but others loved him. People knew Lenny as a tightrope walker that raged against social sickness. Lenny Bruce performed at the Fillmore Auditorium on stage with The Mothers of Invention. He died the following week in Los Angeles.

Above: Lenny Bruce performed his last show at the Fillmore with the Mothers of Invention just a week before his death from a drug overdose.

Timothy Leary

I was told to meet Timothy Leary in Chicago, at the Playboy offices, where he had been invited for a *Playboy* interview. It was to be "a candid conversation with the controversial ex-Harvard professor, prime partisan and prophet of LSD," (*Playboy*, 1966). Leary wore his hair short and was very Ivy League. A forty-seven-year-old man who had not made it at West Point, he was now an eastern preppy, in blue-and-white seersucker jacket, blue button-down shirt, narrow black tie, red socks, and white shoes with red rubber soles. I remember him as always "on," as if he were on speed and trying hard to slow down. He was impatient and frustrated, irritated with those around him because they didn't talk or move at his quick pace. Leary seemed anxious and uncomfortable. After the interview, the plan was to accompany him to the airport and fly on to New York, where a car would take us to the Millbrook mansion. On the plane he read notes from a thick manila envelope. In New York, one of his minions collected us at the airport and we silently drove the two hours to Millbrook.

Arriving at the gated property, we drove through the country darkness, past a long avenue of maples, onto the four-thousand-acre estate owned by New York millionaire William Mellon Hitchcock. More minutes passed before we arrived at a rambling old mansion, with a gatehouse and a covered horse-and-buggy entrance. I half expected a liveried servant to welcome our arrival. The once-elegant, nineteenth-century, turreted,

Ex-Harvard professor Timothy Leary, the prophet of LSD.

sixty-four-room mansion—now a bit down at the heel—made an imposing sight. It was surrounded by a pine forest, tennis courts, open spaces, and meadows. Once we were inside, Leary disappeared without saying a word. I was on my own. Hello?

Strange beginning. After asking different people where I could put my baggage, I was told to take any room upstairs on the second floor that wasn't occupied. Dr. Leary, who had told me to call him Tim, and his assistants occupied the third floor.

Looking around I came upon a well-appointed hotel-size kitchen. Several youngsters were loudly engaged in cooking a large pot of spaghetti. The kitchen was an imposing place for something simple like making a cup of coffee; it was equipped with a wide array of culinary tools, hanging racks of pots and pans of every size, stacked bakery ovens, broilers, a gas range with a dozen burners, and even a pair of walk-in refrigerators. I was impressed. Swinging double doors led out of the kitchen to a pantry. Beyond was a formal dining room with a vaulted ceiling. A fire burned in the stone fireplace and heavy candelabra with thick beeswax candles perfumed the room, providing somber illumination. A gracious ambience filled the house.

The rooms on the main floor were all mahogany paneled, casting a warm glow. A library with a baronial walk-in fireplace was off a grand glass-enclosed solarium. Two brown-and-white goats peeked through French doors.

Top left: Leary's sixty-four-room mansion, Millbrook.
Top right: Dr. Timothy Leary and Mary Ann at Millbrook. This estate, formerly owned by William Mellon Hitchcock, was Leary's headquarters for his organization known as the League for Spiritual Discovery.
Below: The mansion was painted with cubist-like art.

Potted ferns hung over a circular turquoise-and-cream tiled fishpond with water lilies and a water spout; Ionic columns divided spaces into intimate alcoves. Two dozen or more people, ranging from teens to older well-dressed seniors, were sitting around on deep couches, stuffed chairs, and on the thick Persian rugs and parquet floor.

Walking through a crowd in the library, a young woman offered a silver plate with pink sugar cubes. Leary, dressed in a fresh white outfit of Indian madras, had just entered the room and, fending off the overture, explained that I wouldn't be participating in their LSD ritual that night. I was disappointed. A young man and woman trailed Leary, taking notes on steno pads, whenever he had something to say. It was a private ritual and I wasn't invited.

Before the doors closed on me, I could see Leary, sitting cross-legged on a white cushion, the fireplace at his back.

In the hushed room, the fire crackling, Leary's head was bowed and his hands together in an attitude of praying. The messiah of the LSD movement, with his psychedelic pilgrims, was departing for inner space.

Leary was the YMCA summer camp leader at the ritual Friday night bonfire. His exuding sincerity troubled me. I had intruded into a private party. Leary was on his best behavior because the local sheriff of Duchess County, Ralph Quinlan, and G. Gordon Liddy (a district attorney who would later work at the White House) had raided Millbrook and busted Leary on a controlled substance charge. It was later dropped on a technicality. Liddy, at the time, was looking for fame and publicity.

The next day I noticed the aged mansion was in need of paint and garden attention. It had a seedy look by the light of day. Weeds were growing in the middle of the tennis courts, and the once-green lawns and evergreen shrubs were turning brown. The garden hadn't had a watering in weeks except for a vegetable patch next to a chicken coop where a young woman was feeding several ducks and geese. Behind the main house was a cottage in the style of a Swiss chalet—a calm center for cruising space cadets.

Tim Leary espoused eastern thought, including meditation and the martial arts. To him, they were other forms of mind expansion.

Free Clinic

Before the Haight-Ashbury Free Clinic opened its doors in October 1966, at the corner of Cole and Haight Streets, hundreds of young people had few options for medical attention. Dr. David Smith was serving his internship at the University of California Hospital close to the Haight, and his specialty was the study of drug addiction. With the first warnings of the drug problem developing in the Haight-Ashbury, David Smith opened his free clinic.

By this time some of the serious effects of drug addiction and overdose were becoming evident. The hospital's waiting room was known as a "calm center" for spaced-out space pilots, who could go there after finding that whatever drug—usually LSD—they had recently ingested required a guide for their safe return. The Free Clinic offered them help.

A hand-written note pasted to the inside of the front door at the Haight-Ashbury Free Clinic announced, "Calm Center for Bum Trippers is open."

The Haight-Ashbury Free Clinic, started by Dr. David Smith in 1966, offered its services to those suffering from bad acid trips.

Above: **Dr. David Smith, founder of the Haight-Ashbury Free Clinic, and associates.**
Left: **People wait for treatment at the Calm Center.**
Right: **Door to the Free Clinic.**

Calm Center

From the day the Haight-Ashbury Free Clinic opened its front doors in the fall of 1967, it has been full to capacity with patients overflowing the waiting room, called the "Calm Center." During the sixties, the Free Clinic Calm Center was open all night, becoming a crash pad for anyone needing an emergency rest stop. The Free Clinic's specialty has always been the care and treatment of drug addiction.

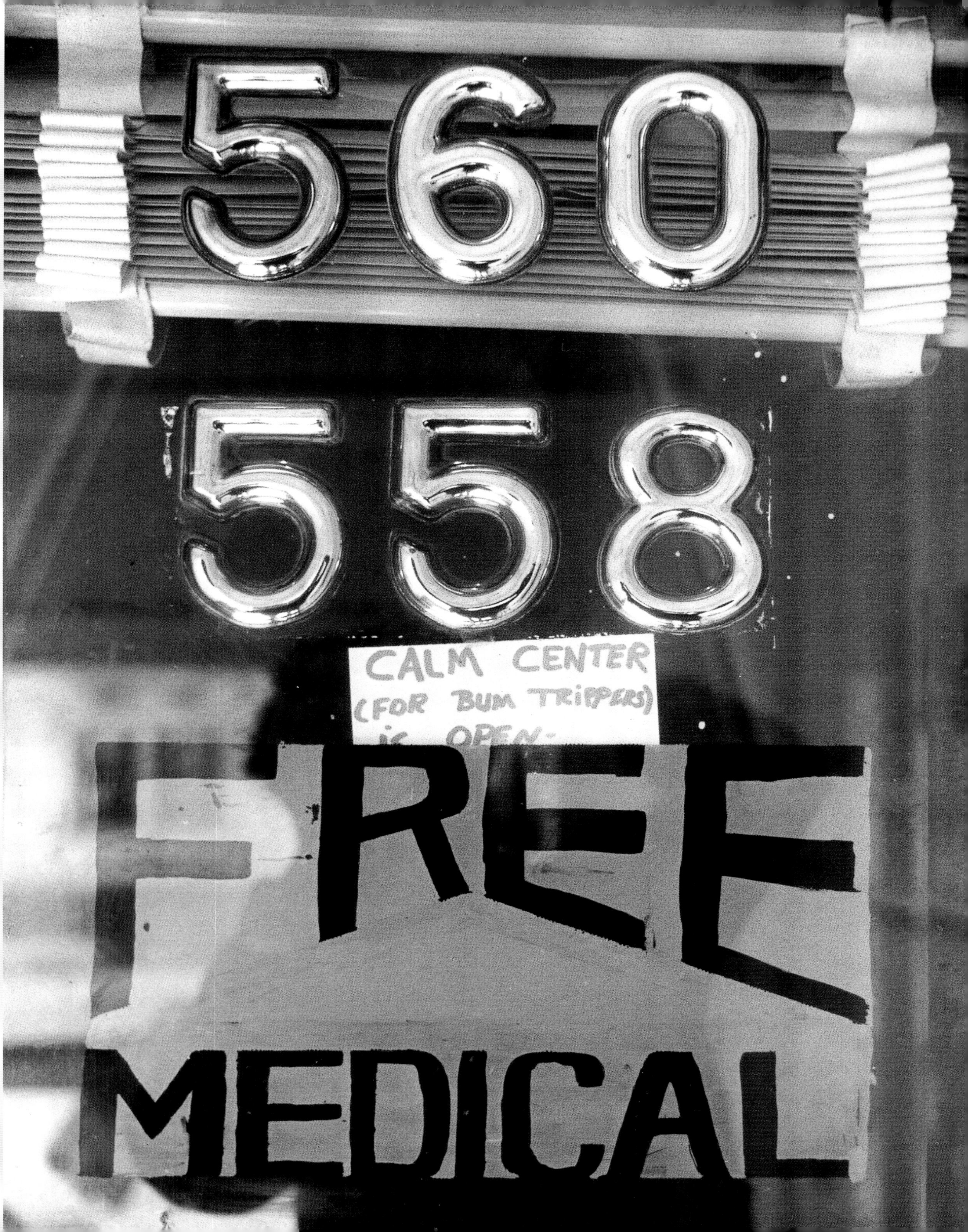
560
558
CALM CENTER
(FOR BUM TRIPPERS)
FREE
MEDICAL

Morning Star Ranch

At the end of a dirt road
just inside the city limits of Santa Rosa,

sixty-five miles north of the Golden Gate, in Sonoma County, is the old Graton Ranch. With thirty-one acres of fruit trees and vegetable gardens, a barn and drying sheds, and a small Victorian house with a wild rose arbor, 12542 Graton Road was the headquarters for the Flower Children's new Shangri-la. It was known as Morning Star, or the Digger Ranch, and was owned by lead folk singer Lou Gottlieb of the Limeliters, a nationally popular musical group of the '50s.

Gottlieb, a tall, lean man with a tropical-looking tan, called his spread Morning Star Ranch and invited the hippies to come live there without restrictions. "Everyone is welcome. There is nothing to fear," he said. He thought about fifty people lived on his land: "The number fluctuates, people come and go, the count isn't exact. This is an experiment in low-cost housing. We have few rules here, no campfires, and no hassles. The people here are the first wave of the technologically unemployables. The cybernation is in its early snowball stage."

The Diggers had a weekly truck run from the ranch to the city, often loaded with strawberries, apples, pears, corn, and squash for their free food program in the Panhandle during '67. But by fall, storm clouds were sighted on the horizon bearing down on the ranch.

Morning Star, or the Digger Ranch, was a nudist colony and a self-proclaimed experiment in low-cost housing.

Several people decided to build more permanent housing and had started a few crude buildings without any construction experience. New arrivals made tent arrangements. That was when the City of Santa Rosa Health Department came out to check on the new neighbors and was shocked to find a trench as their answer to toilet facilities. Also the new construction looked none too safe.

"No!" said the City of Santa Rosa Building Department. New construction must conform to a few rules, number one being a building permit. "Who is in charge?" they demanded while serving legal papers on the residence for a "disorganized camp." Gottlieb's retort was to the effect that the houses under construction were "folk art."

"The neighbors don't like us," intoned Mr. Gottlieb. "They're afraid of us because they say we are guilty of the Socratic crime of corrupting our youth. They also resent the nudity over here. . . . I don't believe in nudism myself; I'd be uncomfortable. And I think everyone should be clothed at the dinner table."

Sonoma County had an ordinance that prohibited the exposure of private parts in the presence of two or more persons of the opposite sex. However, the statute had been preempted by state law, which did not prohibit nudity so long as people in the immediate area did not object.

The final chapter to the Morning Star Ranch saga had Mr. Gottlieb embroiled with various city, county, and state bureaucracies concerning building, sanitation, electrical, health—you name it. Lou Gottlieb was having to endure a full frontal assault. That was when Gottlieb had his epiphany and decided to deed Morning Star Ranch to God.

Bottom left: The Diggers grew vegetables on the ranch for their free food program in the Panhandle.
Left: Morning Star Ranch creator and lead singer with the Limeliters, Lou Gottlieb.
Below: Michael Bowen had a strong influence on the Haight-Ashbury counterculture.

Lou Gottlieb had a school for kids and tried to have Morning Star Ranch become part of the Santa Rosa community. But the ranch's forty to fifty residents were rejected and in the end broke so many laws that the ranch had to close its experiment in community living. Gottlieb finally deeded the ranch to God.

Love Pageant Rally

On the night of September 16, 1966, a tenant in 1090 Page propelled

a coke bottle out of a third floor open window that landed at the feet of two strolling police-men. The culprit was arrested and taken to jail. The hippies protested it as an "illegal bust," and organized a march past the Drogstore Cafe, at the corner of Masonic and Haight. Sitting in a front window of the cafe were Allen Cohen and Michael Bowen, the "Psychedelic Ranger." Allen explained that as he stared after the retreating parade, he had another epiphany. Instead of protesting and always getting a negative response, why not hold a celebration! "If people aren't demonstrating for civil rights violations, it's the war in Vietnam. We should be able to turn some of that negative energy into something more positive."

His epiphany, says Allen, was for a more positive, community-involved protest. He called it the Love Pageant Rally, a celebration to coincide with the moratorium on LSD, October 6, 1966. This celebration would morph as the Human Be-In, two months later.

October 6, 1966 was the date when California outlawed LSD. The drug was seen by the hippies as having mystical elements. October 6, 1966 was equated with "666," found in the Bible, the Cabala, the Masonic, and other mystical orders. It was the sign of "The

The Love Pageant Rally organized people for peace, love, acceptance, understanding, and unity.

Beast." All names for the Antichrist have 666 as their numerical equivalent. A Greek symbol that signified the demonic, the lower mind, also has as its numerical equivalent 666. In the Bible, Revelation 13:18, the Beast was the Roman Empire.

Cohen said, "Instead of protesting the law that was going into effect, our idea was to make a demonstration that

Worldwide Be-In

Perhaps two dozen people who had showed up in their Be-In costumes at Bowen's had found comfortable positions in the meditation room, sharing a peace pipe, waiting till the party began. It started when Allen Ginsberg, trailed by a couple of BBC Television people, tripped in and set up a bright photo light. Ginsberg sat next to Snyder, who was wearing green corduroy jeans and a green blouse blocked with big mauve leaves and flowers. He was waving around a gallon jug of California Bordeaux. "We were invited by Bowen!" offered the television men. Ginsberg groaned.

"I don't know why, but this whole day strikes me as absolutely sane and right and beautiful," one of the men said cheerfully, holding a light meter up to Ginsberg's face. "Michael must have put something in my tea last night."

"What's so insane about a little peace and harmony?" Ginsberg asked him. Part of Ginsberg's entourage was a slight woman, Maretta, who exclaimed, "It was fucking beautiful!" Ginsberg went on, "Like thousands of people would like to come to the park on a day like today. So they can relate to each other as . . . as dharma beings. All sorts of people. Poets, children, even Hell's Angels. People are lonesome. I'm lonesome. It's strange to be in a body. So what I'm doing . . . what we're all doing . . . on a day like today is saying, "Touch me, sleep with me, talk to me."

Bowen came running into the meditation room with a telephone in his hand, and called to Ginsberg that he had Mexico on the line. "In Mexico they meditated with us for six whole hours while we were at the Be-In." Bowen dropped to his knees and began tossing aside pillows until he located a telephone wall socket. "You mean to say you have a phone in your meditation room?" Ginsberg said. "Electric Tibet, baby," said Bowen. "It's like we're bridging the gap between all sorts of people with this—this kind of community festival. I thought it was very Eden-like today, actually. Kind of like Blake's vision of Eden. Music. Babies. People just sort of floating around having a good time and everybody happy and smiling and touching and turning each other on and a lot of groovy chicks all dressed up in their best clothes and . . . "

"But will it last?" asked the television man.

Ginsberg shrugged. "How do I know if it will last?" he said. "And if it doesn't turn out, who cares?"

Conclusion

History is always a matter of looking back—seeking causes, the roots of what is happening in the present. It is also a way in which we can see how others, in the past, have dealt with issues similar to what we are now facing.

The sixties is a good place in history for us to check out. The general populace then was feeling what many are feeling now: tremendously powerless, engulfed in apathy as we grappled with the monster we had created in Vietnam. Our leaders seemed heedless of our wishes, and it took a new generation of young people to show us how corrupted our values had become, and how we could speak out, demonstrate against iniquities...and be heard! The magic of the sixties lay in the power and energy generated by this new generation—a positive power that surged through the world like electric current, affecting not only the United States and its policies, but Europe, and finally piercing the Iron Curtain.

Now, as perhaps never in the years since the sixties, we need to look back for solutions to present problems. We need to shake off our cloaks of powerlessness and apathy. The sixties seem particularly fit for the task. It was magic, and it all really happened!